**COLLEGE OF AEROSPACE DOCTRINE,
RESEARCH AND EDUCATION**

AIR UNIVERSITY

I0424812

Airpower, Afghanistan, and the Future of Warfare
An Alternative View

CRAIG D. WILLS
Lieutenant Colonel, USAF

CADRE Paper No. 25

Originally published by
Air University Press
Maxwell Air Force Base, Alabama 36112-6615

November 2006

Disclaimer

CADRE Papers

CADRE Papers are occasional publications sponsored by the Airpower Research Institute of Air University's College of Aerospace Doctrine, Research and Education (CADRE). Dedicated to promoting the understanding of air and space power theory and application, these studies are published by the Air University Press and broadly distributed to the US Air Force, the Department of Defense and other governmental organizations, leading scholars, selected institutions of higher learning, public-policy institutes, and the media.

All military members and civilian employees assigned to Air University are invited to contribute unclassified manuscripts that deal with air and/or space power history, theory, doctrine or strategy, or with joint or combined service matters bearing on the application of air and/or space power.

Authors should submit three copies of a double-spaced, typed manuscript and an electronic version of the manuscript on removable media along with a brief (200-word maximum) abstract. The electronic file should be compatible with Microsoft Windows and Microsoft Word—Air University Press uses Word as its standard word-processing program.

Please send inquiries or comments to
Chief of Research
Airpower Research Institute
CADRE
401 Chennault Circle
Maxwell AFB AL 36112-6428
Tel: (334) 953-5508
DSN 493-5508
Fax: (334) 953-6739
DSN 493-6739
E-mail: cadre.research@maxwell.af.mil

Contents

Tables

Foreword

It is helpful to view current applications of American airpower in two operational mediums. On the one hand, aircraft and tactics have provided a high certainty of air superiority against enemy fighters. On the other hand, American airpower has reached new levels of effectiveness with night-and-day, all-weather, stealth, and precision bombing sustained with surprisingly sensitive surveillance-and-reconnaissance capabilities for target identification and battle damage assessment. The enforcement of the "no-fly zones" over Iraq, known as Operations Northern and Southern Watch, during the 1990s—as well as the wars in Bosnia, Operation Allied Force in 1999; in Afghanistan, Operation Enduring Freedom in 2001; and in Iraq, Operation Iraqi Freedom in 2003—highlighted the singular effectiveness of airpower to predominate in some joint and combined forms of war. Lt Col Craig D. Wills examines this rather new application of airpower in the long-running history of direct support of ground combat operations—an activity long declared by thoughtful Airmen as doctrinally unsuitable for airpower. Now it seems that this air support to the ground forces can be considered a core mission function. How times have changed.

Wills argues that the twentieth-century argument between air and ground proponents has changed significantly since the Gulf War, and it comes down to the relative importance of the ground or air in the mix. It is more than just using air as a supporting component to the ground forces—if this is true, current force organization and employment is adequate. However, if the air predominates in combat operations, then, as Wills puts it in his first chapter, joint operations doctrine needs to be rethought. A changed balance "will affect the military at every level . . . force structure, organization, weapons acquisition, doctrine, and training" (p. 3). Notwithstanding the blunt commentary from ground proponents, Wills offers that airpower has come to dominate air/ground relations.

This is demonstrated, he says, by three factors. First, no adversary can mass without great destruction by precision-strike airpower; second, this lethality is the most politically attractive weapon in America's arsenal because it is discriminate; and third, this is doubly attractive because it is so inexpensive, especially for political leadership.

In several chapters, the author explains why airpower is so different in the twenty-first century, showing how airpower has changed land combat. The most dramatic illustration is the new combination of air, special forces, and local or indigenous troops that can, in many instances, defeat larger and better-equipped forces. This kind of "force intensification" preserves combat power and American lives. Such a remarkable increase in the capability of airpower changes the dynamics of American warfare and therefore needs to be recognized in doctrine and force structure.

Airpower, Afghanistan, and the Future of Warfare: An Alternative View was written as a master's thesis in the 2004–05 class for the Air University's School of Advanced Air and Space Studies (SAASS), Maxwell AFB, Alabama. Colonel Wills's study was chosen as one of the best of its group. The College of Aerospace Doctrine, Research and Education (CADRE) is pleased to publish this SAASS research as a CADRE Paper and thereby make it available to a wider audience within the US Air Force and beyond.

DANIEL R. MORTENSEN
Chief of Research
Airpower Research Institute, CADRE

About the Author

Lt Col Craig D. Wills was commissioned through the Reserve Officer Training Corps in 1990. In 1992 he completed Specialized Undergraduate Navigator Training at Mather Air Force Base (AFB), California, and was selected for follow-on training in the F-15E. After a tour at Royal Air Force Lakenheath, United Kingdom, Colonel Wills was selected for Undergraduate Pilot Training, which he completed in 1996. After two tours in the F-15C, he reported to Air University, Maxwell AFB, Alabama. In May 2004, Colonel Wills was assigned to Seventh Air Force, Osan Air Base, Republic of Korea, where he served as the director of the Air Force Strategy Division. Colonel Wills is currently the operations officer of the 493d Fighter Squadron "Grim Reapers" at Royal Air Force Lakenheath, United Kingdom.

Acknowledgments

The luxurious lifestyle of Air University would not be possible were it not for the dedicated men and women who take up the slack in the line while a few lucky officers attend school. I would like to thank the fighting men and women of the United States military who carried my load, fighting and winning two wars during my time in school.

Special thanks are due my thesis advisors, Prof. Richard Andres and Col Thomas E. Griffith Jr. Their constant enthusiasm, intellectual acumen, and dedication were (and are) a source of inspiration for me. Thanks also to Col Tom Ehrhard, retired, for his early support of this project.

My deepest thanks remain for my incredible wife Britt and our two wonderful daughters, Brooke and Audrey, for their love, patience, and support during this busy year—no man could hope for a finer family. Finally, I would like to thank the members of "Lucky 13" who exemplify the best that America has to offer: good luck and Godspeed!

Abstract

The "Future of Warfare" means increasing the emphasis on air support to the joint fight. The USAF continues to promote the importance of air superiority, acquiring aircraft and training pilots to attain air dominance. American Airmen do not want a long engagement to gain air superiority in the event of battle with a major power. On the other hand, American airpower has reached new levels of effectiveness with night-and-day, all-weather, stealth, and precision bombing sustained with surprisingly sensitive surveillance-and-reconnaissance capabilities for target identification and battle damage assessment. The enforcement of the "no-fly zones" over Iraq, known as Operations Northern and Southern Watch, during the 1990s—as well as the wars in Bosnia, Operation Allied Force in 1999; in Afghanistan, Operation Enduring Freedom in 2001; and in Iraq, Operation Iraqi Freedom in 2003—highlighted the singular effectiveness of airpower to predominate in some joint and combined forms of war. Lt Col Craig D. Wills examines this rather new application of airpower in the long-running history of direct support of ground-combat operations—an activity long declared by thoughtful Airmen as doctrinally unsuitable for airpower. Now it seems that this air support to ground forces can be considered a core mission function.

Wills maintains that the twentieth-century argument between air and ground proponents has changed significantly since the Gulf War and that it comes down to the relative importance of the ground or air in the mix. It is more than just using air as a supporting component to the ground forces—if this is true, current force organization and employment are adequate. However, if the air predominates in combat operations, then, as Wills puts it in his first chapter, joint-operations doctrine needs to be rethought. A changed balance "will affect the military at every level . . . force structure, organization, weapons acquisition, doctrine, and training" (p. 3).

Notwithstanding the blunt commentary from ground proponents, Wills offers that airpower has come to dominate air/ground relations. This is demonstrated, he says, by three factors. First, no adversary can mass without great destruction by precision-strike airpower; second, this lethality is the most politically attractive weapon in America's arsenal because it is discriminate; and third, this is doubly attractive because it is so inexpensive, especially for political leadership.

In his first chapter, the author explains why airpower is so different in the twenty-first century and how it has changed land combat. The most dramatic example is the new combination of air, special forces, and local or indigenous troops that can, in many instances, defeat larger and better-equipped forces. This kind of "force intensification" preserves combat power and American lives. Such a remarkable increase in the capability of airpower changes the dynamics of American warfare and therefore needs to be recognized in doctrine and force structure. If, as some ground components argue, airpower is best used as a supporting component to the ground, then no new force reorganization is required. Some ground supporters dwell on the overstated proclamations of Billy Mitchell and Hugh Trenchard that held airpower capable of winning war unaided. The argument is not common among current airpower leaders. Ground spokesmen today also highlight failures of airpower to dominate in urban situations, and they critique the move towards lighter ground forces. Wills recognizes the importance of ground forces to concentrate the enemy, to shape the battlefield for application of airpower. He argues for a shift that emphasizes airpower and uses smaller, more-powerful land forces in an efficient manner.

In the second chapter, the author lays out specific developments that make airpower of this century fundamentally different than it was in earlier decades. The attractiveness to political leaders is clearly outlined. Chapter three offers evidence that with a changed capability, national leaders have greater political utility with airpower. Chapter four emphasizes recent operational examples, especially use of special forces as well as airpower's ability to deliver more effective firepower to operate as though it were a much bigger force. Finally, the last chapter makes an argument to change doctrine along with military force structure, one that truly reflects airpower's ascendance in the air/ground relationship.

Chapter 1

Framing the Debate

In order to assure an adequate national defense, it is necessary—and sufficient—to be in a position in case of war to conquer the command of the air.

—Giulio Douhet

America's reliance on air power has set the American way of war apart from all others for well over half a century. Other countries might field doughty infantry-men, canny submariners, or scientific artillerists comparable in skill and numbers to our own. The United States alone, however, has engaged in a single-minded and successful quest for air superiority in every conflict it has fought since World War I. Air warfare remains the distinctively American form of warfare—high tech, cheap in American lives lost, and (at least in theory) quick. From the point of view of America's enemies, past, current, and potential, air power seems the distinctively American form of military intimidation.

—Eliot Cohen

Less than two decades after the flights at Kitty Hawk, Giulio Douhet asserted, "To conquer the command of the air means victory; to be beaten in the air means defeat and acceptance of whatever terms the enemy may be pleased to impose."[1] Some Airmen disagree with this dictum, but most accept the assertion that airpower is a vital part of modern war. Indeed, warfare in the twentieth century proved that Douhet was at least partly right; nations holding air superiority have rarely lost a conventional war.

Since World War II, the potential of airpower has grown at an incredible rate, and now, for the first time in airpower history, Airmen can reliably hit their targets. In 1944, for example, over 1,000 B-17 sorties were typically required to destroy a single target. Today, a B-2 can strike and conceivably destroy 16 different targets in a single sortie.[2] The Norden bombsight has given way to munitions aided by lasers and the global positioning system (GPS). Reconnaissance aircraft, satellites, and unmanned aerial vehicles (UAV) patrol the heavens searching for targets while command and control aircraft continuously pass accurate targeting information to strike aircraft.

Many view airpower's newfound lethality as an opportunity to finally fulfill the dream of early air theorists like Douhet: to destroy an enemy quickly and completely, relying solely on airpower. This tantalizing notion obscures what may possibly be a more relevant development. Recent combat in Iraq, Kosovo, and Afghanistan suggests that airpower has enabled relatively small numbers of ground forces to defeat significantly more-powerful opponents. This represents an important change in the nature of joint warfare, one that has profound implications for the United States.

Research Question

This paper seeks to examine how the relationship between air and "ground power" is changing. "Relationship" refers not simply to the interaction between these two forms of force application but to the synergistic effects of airpower and ground power in the service of national security. To quantify these effects, two questions are asked. First, which form of force application provides the most significant contribution to achieving US military objectives? Second, which form of force application is best able to meet US political objectives at costs acceptable to policy makers?

Though political considerations and military effectiveness may seem unrelated, these interlace in a world where political constraints on the use of force seem to be increasing. Although nuclear weapons are clearly more powerful (militarily effective) than conventional munitions, political restrictions preclude their use under most circumstances. If application of a particular weapon carries prohibitive political consequences, it is actually not available for use, and decision makers must consider other options. Any discussion of the relative utility of air and ground power must include an examination of the political considerations attendant to the actual use of air forces and ground forces. Moreover, as Carl von Clausewitz observed over a century ago, "The political object is the goal, war is the means of reaching it, and means can never be considered in isolation from their purpose."[3]

Relevance

If airpower is best used as a supporting component to ground forces, then there is no need to alter the current models of force organization and employment. If, however, airpower has grown dominant in the air/ground relationship, there are unavoidable implications for US foreign and defense policies. To be sure, America's unquestioned military superiority promises few penalties for remaining wedded to old paradigms. However, recent advances in airpower capability may offer important alternatives. Is it now possible to ask how to maximize the effectiveness of airpower? Asking the question does not mean the obviation of ground forces, but it does offer the possibility of greater efficiency in force application, less close combat, and fewer casualties due to friendly fire.

Acceptance of a changed balance between air and ground power will affect the military at every level. Areas such as US force structure, organization, weapons acquisition, doctrine, and training may be subject to reassessment. Naturally, such issues involve addressing service budgets and, perhaps more importantly, changing service.

The Airpower Debate

Operation Desert Storm kindled renewed interest in the question of airpower effectiveness. Perhaps the core issue is the exact nature of airpower's contribution to victory. Debate over this issue stagnated as extremists in each camp hurriedly claimed "decisiveness" for their preferred form of warfare. Airpower's success in the Gulf War coincided with the demise of the Soviet Union, and there has been increasing pressure on ground-power proponents to justify the existence of a large army—a difficult task in an era characterized by absence of a clear threat to American interests.

Some have also offered unqualified, absolute views regarding airpower's capability. Air Force historian Richard Davis noted, "Strategic and tactical air power together constituted the decisive factor in the Coalition's quick and almost bloodless victory in the Persian Gulf."[4] Richard Hallion famously opined, "Simply (if boldly) stated, air power won the Gulf War."[5] The Army, not to be outdone, asserted, "As part of the Coalition, the American Army decisively defeated the fourth largest field army in the world. It did so at the lowest cost in human life ever recorded for a conflict of such magnitude."[6] Daryl Press similarly opined, "Airpower was neither necessary nor sufficient for victory in the Gulf War."[7]

Very few sought a balanced approach, and the argument only intensifies when tight budgetary decisions are in the offing. All this bickering resulted in a stalled airpower debate. As Benjamin Lambeth lamented, "There surely must be more imaginative ways of thinking about the changing relationship between air and land power than simply in reductionist either-or terms."[8]

The Proairpower Camp

Recently, several authors have suggested a new relationship between air and ground power. In 1993 a RAND study chartered to examine the role of airpower in joint operations concluded: "The results of our analysis do indicate that the calculus has changed and airpower's ability to contribute to the joint battle has increased."[9] Eliot Cohen, director of the *Gulf War Air Power Survey*, commented, "Whether this remarkable outcome presages a new relationship between air forces and ground forces will, no doubt, be debated for years to come. . . . But if air power again exerts similar dominance over opposing ground forces, the conclusion will be inescapable that some threshold in the relationship between air and ground forces was first crossed in Desert Storm."[10] Maj William Dries, an Air Force graduate of the Army's elite School of Advanced Military Studies, argued for "a new way of thinking about land maneuver and fires." Dries asserted that in certain cases, land power should be used to "make enemy action predictable and enemy positions known and therefore . . . susceptible to aerial attack."[11] Finally, Anthony Cordesman found that "the Afghan conflict has shown that a combination of precision . . . coupled with greatly improved intelligence and targeting systems can, in some contingencies, provide much of the heavy firepower that previously had to be provided with artillery and armor."[12]

In spite of these favorable views of airpower, its proponents have traditionally stopped short of endorsing a wholesale change in the air/ground relationship. Their assertions focused too narrowly on the question of "decisiveness" or are qualified in the interest of presenting a less controversial view.[13]

The Argument for the Status Quo

Billy Mitchell, Douhet, and Hugh Trenchard died over a half century ago, yet Airmen continue to be held accountable for their extreme claims. Max Boot, although complimentary of recent air successes, complained, "The air force still has not realized the dreams of Giulio Douhet, Billy Mitchell and other early advocates of airpower, who claimed that aerial bombardment could win wars by itself."[14] Such viewpoints are mere straw men. No Air Force leader in recent history has argued that air alone will routinely win wars.

Another common tactic for those who view air as merely an adjunct to ground forces is to criticize tactical limitations of airpower. Retired US Marine general and veteran of the Vietnam and Desert Storm wars, Paul Van Riper apparently faulted airpower for being unable to find a notional "enemy company in the basement of a built up area" or "the twelve terrorists mixed with that crowd in the village market."[15] Lt Col Timothy Reese suggested that politicians may become so enamored with precision-guided munitions (PGM) that they fail to develop adequate strategy and characterize the PGMs as "dangerous" and "seductive" in nature.[16] Stephen Biddle observes that in Afghanistan:

in the Qala-e-Gangi fortress uprising, the renegade prisoners were quickly driven out of the above-ground prison yard and isolated in a handful of small underground chambers whose locations and perimeter were well-known. These were then pounded by allied airpower: entire ammunition payloads of multiple AC-130 gunships and no fewer than seven 2,000-pound JDAMs [joint direct attack munition] were expended against this tiny area. Yet the defenders survived and continued to resist until succumbing only to the medieval technology of flooding by cold water.[17]

Such arguments are often used to reinforce a common theme—sweeping changes in Army force structure are risky, even dangerous. William Hawkins contends that it is difficult to rapidly upgrade light forces designed for the low end of the conflict spectrum to heavy forces designed for larger wars, which usually have much higher stakes.[18] At their core, comments like those of Reese and Hawkins are simple fear mongering, designed to obfuscate the accomplishments of airpower and stall the debate, rather than advance it.

I hope to elevate the airpower debate. Airpower has evolved so much that a much more dramatic change is afoot. It is time to stop arguing over minor tactical limitations and start working the proper relationship between air and ground power.

My Argument

I argue that airpower has come to dominate the air/ground relationship. Three main factors demonstrate that air now dominates ground power. First, and most importantly, precision-strike airpower has fundamentally changed the nature of land combat. No adversary can mass against friendly ground forces without facing certain destruction. Second, airpower's lethality has made it the most politically useful military tool in America's arsenal. Finally, as a natural extension of its lethality, airpower can provide policymakers and commanders alike with the option to use fewer ground troops to accomplish a given objective. Operations Enduring Freedom and Iraqi Freedom (OEF and OIF) demonstrated that in the presence of precision-strike airpower, fewer forces are required during the ground-combat phase of modern war.

Future enemies are unlikely to mass; instead, they will disperse and conceal, engaging in tactics of the weak. This phenomenon means that there will be a permanent need for effective ground forces. In the future, ground power will routinely be employed to force the enemy out of concealed positions, thus effectively shaping the battlefield for application of airpower. This reversal of roles will serve to destroy or neutralize the enemy more efficiently while simultaneously reducing friendly casualties.

America must shift more capability to airpower and utilize land power in a more efficient manner. Current experiences in Iraq show that as long as invasion and occupation remain viable foreign policy options, the US Army is as small as it should be. This does not mitigate the Department of Defense's (DOD) responsibility to transform the Army, however. Boots on the ground are critical to success, but it is vital that America decide how many and what kind of boots to deploy. The Army must utilize the efficiencies gained through airpower to embrace missions such as peace enforcement and peacekeeping. It is time to disabuse ourselves of the notion that preparing for war is the same as preparing for peace. Land forces must be organized, trained, and equipped for peacekeeping and nation-building missions with the same high competency with which they conduct warfare.

Finally, the services must develop appropriate doctrine, strategies, and training to maximize the synergy of this new relationship. The American military must not allow itself to stagnate in this era of superiority. Lessons learned over the past decade must be codified in doctrine lest they be forgotten; an error that might prove costly to America in both blood and treasure.

The Road Ahead

Chapter 2 explains the specific developments that make airpower of the twenty-first century fundamentally different than it was 20 or even 10 years ago. Chapter 3 offers evidence that airpower has changed the face of land combat and now gives national leaders greater political utility than does ground power. Chapter 4 analyzes the combination of special operations forces (SOF) and airpower to illustrate that precision airpower is allowing comparatively small forces to achieve effects disproportionate to their size. Chapter 5 explores the implications of airpower's ascendancy, arguing that military force structure, doctrine, and transformation must reflect airpower's ascendance in the air/ground relationship.

Notes

(All notes appear in shortened form. For full details, see the appropriate entry in the bibliography.)

1. Douhet, *Command of the Air*, 28.
2. Deptula, *Effects-Based Operations*, 8.

3. Clausewitz, *On War*, 87.

4. Cited in Myers, *Joint Aerospace Power.*

5. Hallion, *Storm over Iraq*, 1.

6. Scales, *Certain Victory*, 5.

7. Press, "Myth of Airpower," 7.

8. Lambeth, *Transformation of American Air Power*, 312.

9. Bowie et al., *New Calculus*, xxi.

10. Keaney and Cohen, *Gulf War Air Power Survey*, 246–47.

11. Dries, "Future Counterland Operations," 50. Dries and his monograph advisor Lt Col James Cody are both Air Force officers.

12. Cordesman, *Lessons of Afghanistan*, 16.

13. Lambeth's appraisal aims to advance a moderate view of airpower. See his *Transformation of American Air Power*. Similarly, Keaney and Cohen and Major Dries suggest that a new air/ground relationship "may" be in the offing. See also Keaney and Cohen, *Gulf War Air Power Survey*; and Dries, "Future Counterland Operations."

14. Boot, "New American Way of War," 55.

15. Cited in Lambeth, *Transformation of American Air Power*, 301.

16. Reese, "Precision Firepower," 46–53. Reese is the director of the Army's Cavalry Proponency Office.

17. Biddle, "Afghanistan," 35.

18. Hawkins, "What Not to Learn," 24–32.

Chapter 2

Airpower, War, and Diplomacy

Today air power is the dominant factor in war. It may not win a war by itself alone, but without it no major war can be won.

—Adm Arthur Radford, 1951

Operations in Iraq ushered in an era of unprecedented growth in airpower capabilities. Although the Army and Air Force remain inextricably linked, airpower has become so capable that it cannot be viewed as simply an enabling force for ground commanders. In fact evidence suggests that the relationship has reversed. Today airpower dominates the air/ground relationship due to two simple realities: (1) an increase in the physical capability of airpower to achieve effects on the battlefield and (2) geopolitical circumstances that ensure airpower will increasingly be the most useful form of force application for US decision makers. The greatest improvements have been in the area of the physical capabilities of airpower.

Physical Improvements

Perhaps the most important improvement in airpower capability since World War II is the development of PGMs. Since the days of the Wright brothers, Airmen have dreamed of bombing their enemy and achieving decisive effects in war. The grand visions of Douhet, Trenchard, and Mitchell long outpaced the ability of airmen to hit what they were aiming at. Despite claims of Air Corps Tactical School enthusiasts, bombers were only rarely able to hit a "pickle barrel" in the 1930s and then only under ideal circumstances.[1] Experiences in World War II proved that such ideal bombing conditions rarely exist in combat. Air attack during World War II was rarely "precise." Postwar surveys found that only about 20 percent of the bombs dropped fell within 1,000 feet of their intended targets.[2] Airpower failed to deliver on the more grandiose claims of early theorists in

9

World War II. Although airmen clearly made a significant contribution to victory, the nature and relative value of that contribution remains hotly contested.

Since World War II, the airpower debate has progressed little, but bombs and missiles have become steadily more accurate. The later stages of the Vietnam War saw the unveiling of the laser-guided bomb (LGB), but it was not until Desert Storm that the LGB was employed to full effect. Infrared targeting systems and the LGBs on aircraft such as the F-117, F-111F, and F-15E combined with terrain-mapping cruise missiles to usher in a new era of precision. Images of Tomahawk cruise missiles launching off ships in the Persian Gulf and bombs penetrating ventilation shafts in Baghdad introduced the world to the improved lethality of modern airpower. The LGBs demonstrated tremendous precision during the Gulf War, achieving average accuracies within 10 meters circular error probable (CEP) with many weapons hitting the proverbial pickle barrel.

Maj Gen David Deptula, a major architect of the Desert Storm air campaign, notes that one stealth fighter delivering two LGBs on target effectively has the equivalent firepower of 1,000 B-17 sorties during World War II.[3] During Desert Storm only three weapon systems were capable of delivering the PGMs, none of which were heavy bombers. Although precision-weapons video dominated nightly television footage, in reality such weapons constituted only 7 percent of all bombs delivered during the war.[4] Desert Storm also highlighted a key weakness of the LGBs—their inaccuracy during poor weather allows enemy forces a sanctuary during the air campaign.

In the years since Desert Storm, precision technology has grown to include weapons which leverage America's space superiority. Weapons such as the JDAM utilize the GPS for guidance and are therefore less susceptible to poor weather. Although not as accurate as the LGBs in good weather, the JDAMs allow accuracies within 10–15 meters even when dropping through solid cloud decks.[5] This effectively removes the opportunity to use weather to conceal movement. Operation Allied Force showcased this new ability to target accurately through weather. Unfortunately only the B-2 was capable of delivering the JDAMs, thus the poor weather that prevailed in the Balkans and marginalized the air campaign because of the consequent lack of the PGM capability.

The USAF has responded to this limitation by taking steps to ensure that nearly all of its ground-attack aircraft are capable of delivering the JDAMs to the extent that it is even considering modifying air-to-air F-15s to deliver these munitions. The weapons capacity of the B-2 is undergoing expansions that will upgrade its weapons-carrying capacity, allowing each of the heavy bombers to deliver as many as eighty 500-pound JDAMs or the equivalent of 20,000 B-17 sorties during World War II.[6] The USAF recently fielded an upgraded weapon by combining the all-weather capability of the JDAMs with the precision of the LGBs, adding new flexibility to the air component and ensuring accuracy regardless of environmental conditions.[7]

The latest conflicts in Afghanistan and in Iraq illustrate the USAF's commitment to precision. In each of these conflicts, the percentage of precision munitions has increased, finally amounting to nearly 70 percent of the total tonnage dropped in OIF (table 1). Airpower thus continues to become increasingly precise with almost every sortie "destroying" its target(s).

Table 1. Weapons data for recent major military operations

Military Operation	Weapons			Percentage	
	Total	Precision[a]	All-WX[b]	Precision	All-WX[c]
Desert Storm	265,000	20,450	333	8	0.1/ 2
Allied Force	23,000	8,050	985	35	4/12
Enduring Freedom[d]	22,000	12,500	7,300	57	33/58
Iraqi Freedom[e]	29,199	19,948	9,645	68	33/48

Source: Kenneth Tatum, "The Impact of All-Weather Precision on Escalation Dominance" (student paper, School of Advanced Air and Space Studies, Maxwell AFB, AL, 2003), 4.

[a]Precision weapons include the LGBs, Mavericks, AGM-130s, Hellfires, and all of the All-WX weapons.

[b]All-WX weapons include the Tomahawk land-attack missile (TLAM), enhanced guided bomb unit (EGBU), JDAM, high-speed antiradiation missile (HARM), joint standoff weapon (JSOW), and wind corrected munitions dispenser (WCMD).

[c]All-WX percentages are of Total/Percentage of Precision.

[d]All data is estimated as of April 2002.

[e]Data is current through 18 April 2003.

The unveiling of the Stealth Fighter in November 1988 portended a second significant development in the rise of American airpower. Stealth technology enables F-117 and B-2 aircraft to penetrate the most sophisticated air defenses in the world with virtual impunity. This remarkable technology proved its worth during Desert Storm when F-117s flew less than 2 percent of the combat sorties and attacked over 40 percent of the targets on the master-target list—suffering no losses in the process.[8] Stealth is invisibility in tactical terms. The strategic meaning of stealth is defeat of enemy air defenses. The heavy B-52 losses during Linebacker II in Vietnam, the collection of F-105 parts on "Thud Ridge," and Israeli experiences in the Yom Kippur War illustrate the difficulty of attacking heavily defended areas using nonstealthy assets.[9] The first assets used in war, stealth weapon systems will play the crucial role of "kicking down the door" for other platforms and components.

Another important transformation in airpower's physical capability is in the area of persistence. Perhaps the most valid traditional criticism of airpower is that it usually has been a transient on the battlefield. Aircraft proved extremely effective when available, but too often they lacked the range, loiter time, or all-weather capability. These limitations were seldom lost on an enemy. Adolf Hitler directed that his 1944 Ardennes offensive take place during foul weather to neutralize Allied air.[10] The weather lifted, however, and Allied air forces attacked with zeal; turning the tide in the Battle of the Bulge. While the battle ended on a positive note, airpower still had provided relatively little support to Allied soldiers locked in mortal combat during that bitter winter of 1944.

Today, airpower can be very persistent over the battlefield. Aerial refueling enables even short-range fighters to maintain significant time-on-station and at great distances from home bases. In the Korean War, aircraft operating from distant bases in Japan lacked sufficient endurance to provide ground forces with reliable support. By contrast during Operation Anaconda in OEF, fighter aircraft routinely operated from bases 700 miles from the battlefield. One F-15E crew flew a record 15-hour mission in support of troops on the ground, and B-2 crews routinely flew nonstop from the United States to attack targets in Afghanistan—often remaining on station for several hours at a time.[11] The UAVs—also highly persistent—are becoming increasingly important to air warfare. New intelligence, surveillance, and reconnaissance (ISR) platforms such as the Predator and Global Hawk are able to stay aloft for over 24 hours at a time, ensuring that enemies of the future will have few opportunities to reposition forces without fear of detection—a capability exploited in the most recent war with Iraq.[12]

A fierce desert sandstorm tested the air component's staying power during OIF. As the storm intensified, elements of several Iraqi Republican Guard divisions attempted to advance to engage coalition forces. Blowing sand wreaked havoc on coalition infrared sensors but had no effect on Global Hawk, the joint surveillance target attack radar system (JSTARS), and certain defense satellite systems that utilize nearly weatherproof, synthetic aperture radar. As a result, "Coalition planners were receiving a virtually uninterrupted stream of data from JSTARS, Global Hawk systems, and from advanced satellites."[13] Coalition bombers attacked the Iraqis using the all-weather JDAMs, nearly "obliterating Saddam Hussein's premier ground forces."[14] Even in close air support (CAS), typically hampered by poor weather, airpower proved very responsive. At the height of the storm, B-52s and B-1s dropped the JDAMs in direct support of the Army's 7th Cavalry and halted an Iraqi counterattack near the town of Najaf.[15]

The UAVs, tankers, and space surveillance platforms have combined to deflate the argument that airpower is merely transient over the battlefield. Physical improvements in airpower's capability to achieve effects on the modern battlefield have clearly increased dramatically. Improvements in precision, stealth, and persistence ensure that airpower is more lethal and survivable than ever. These qualities produce a concomitant increase in the political usefulness of airpower, a subject addressed in the next section.

Political Factors in the Rise of Airpower

Decisions to use military force rarely depend purely on calculations of military effectiveness. Popularly elected leaders must make decisions with an eye on political ramifications, particularly in the United States. Pressures on elected officials continue to intensify, spurred by phenomena such as 24-hour satellite news, the Internet, and globalization. These techno-social factors often and quickly

13

rearrange the political context in which leaders make decisions regarding the use of military force. In the rapidly evolving world of politics, airpower helps leaders control political risk by minimizing casualties, offering nearly instantaneous military options, and achieving strategic effects without major commitments.

For decades American political leaders have demonstrated a decreasing willingness to commit military force in political situations that entail the risk of significant casualties.[16] Airpower offers leaders a strong military option without the attendant risk of large-scale, friendly casualties. The inherently smaller number of military personnel at risk combined with increasingly accurate PGMs assures that the numbers of casualties during an air action will likely be low.

Critics lament the "no ground invasion" policy during the North Atlantic Treaty Organization's (NATO) 1999 conflict with Serbia as a manifestation of this casualty aversion. Considering NATO's inability to stop the Serbian slaughter of Albanian Kosovar refugees, it seems likely that using ground troops in Kosovo would have prevented considerable loss of life. The harsh reality is that leaders must enjoy public support to stay in office. Military and strategic decisions will always be made with consideration of public support, and high numbers of casualties are likely to lead to a decrease in that support. In the case of Kosovo, the public demanded US military action to stop the slaughter of thousands of Albanian Kosovars but not at the cost of American casualties. Airpower provided the leadership with an opportunity to take assertive action with little risk to friendly forces. The remarkable fact that America suffered no casualties during the 78-day action underscores airpower's unique ability to mitigate political risk.

The inherent flexibility of airpower also makes it an attractive choice for civilian leadership. Airpower's ability to project force to any corner of the globe is unrivalled by other instruments of national power. The United States has acquired the ability to strike anywhere on the planet with conventional munitions. Long-range bomber missions from the continental United States (CONUS), once considered novel, have become routine. This unprecedented ability to hold would-be aggressors at constant risk is a vital tool in America's strategic and diplomatic arsenal and represents another factor in airpower's ascendancy in relation to ground power.

Finally airpower offers governments the ability to create strategic effects without major commitments of military force. As Thomas A. Keaney and Eliot Cohen noted, "Air power is an unusually seductive form of military strength because, like modern courtship, it appears to offer the pleasures of gratification without the burdens of commitment."[17] The 1982 Israeli raid on Iraq's Osirak nuclear facility, for example, created a desirable strategic effect but did not lead to a wider war. The US raid on Libya in 1986 accomplished the desired goal of demonstrating US resolve but did not lead to a significant commitment of US ground forces. Operation Deliberate Force in 1995 demonstrated NATO's resolve in the Balkans without significantly escalating the alliance's involvement.

Deployment of ground forces represents a major step that Americans are usually hesitant to take, even when the stakes are very high—as in the case of Rwanda. Hundreds of thousands died because America was unwilling to commit soldiers or marines. America's apparent aversion to casualties is a clear historical trend that is unlikely to change. Force-employment options that entail large deployments of soldiers and marines increase the chances of significant American casualties and can create a perceived political risk for leadership. Civilian decision makers will continue to turn to military options that create quick strategic effects without large-scale deployment. Airpower will provide leaders the most viable option to satisfy these requirements. Clausewitz's assertion that "war is nothing but the continuation of policy by other means" ensures that airpower will continue to be a first choice for decision makers.[18]

A Changing Relationship

Recent improvements in airpower's physical capabilities and its political usefulness have driven airpower's ascendancy in the air/ground relationship. A series of case studies follows that illustrates several propositions concerning airpower today:

- Where America enjoys air superiority, her adversaries cannot mass without facing almost certain destruction.

- Airpower's lethality makes it the most politically useful military tool in America's arsenal.

- Airpower is reducing the need for large numbers of ground troops during the combat phase of modern war.

Notes

1. Legend has it that in the early days of aviation, pilots boasted of marksmanship that would allow them to hit a pickle barrel from high altitude. Since then the term *pickle* has evolved in fighter aviation to denote the release of missiles or bombs against their targets.

2. *United States Strategic Bombing Surveys*, 13.

3. Deptula, *Effects-Based Operations*, 8.

4. Rip and Hasik, *Precision Revolution*, 224.

5. Ibid., 236.

6. This calculation assumes that 2,000 pounds of high explosives are required to kill a target. Each B-2 could destroy 20 targets or 10 times the number that one F-117 could destroy (equal to 600 F-4 sorties in Vietnam or 20,000 B-17 sorties). See Deptula, *Effects-Based Operations*, 8, for sortie-comparison numbers.

7. The EGBU-27 is a hybrid weapon, utilizing both GPS and laser guidance for optimum precision.

8. Deptula, *Effects-Based Operations*, 10.

9. The F-105 "Thud" flew some of the most difficult missions against North Vietnam. The enemy shot down many F-105s near a ridge north of Hanoi used for navigation and terrain masking from enemy radar—hence the term *Thud Ridge*.

10. Parker, *To Win the Winter Sky*, 1.

11. Grant, "War Nobody Expected," 20; and Grant, *Afghan Air War*, 15. B-2 sortie details derived from the author's interview of Maj Melvin "Sideshow" Deaile (Maxwell AFB, AL, January 2004). Deaile's sortie is reportedly the longest US combat sortie on record: 34 hours en route from the CONUS to Afghanistan, seven hours "in country," then three hours en route to Diego Garcia, culminating in approximately 45 hours of flight time.

12. Global Hawk, for example, boasts a range of 14,000 nautical miles and endurance of up to 42 hours. In practical terms, this equates to the capability to commute from New York to Los Angeles, loiter for 24 hours, and then return to New York. During the loiter time, the Global Hawk will conduct surveillance over an area of 40,000 square miles or roughly the portion of the state of California from Santa Barbara to the Mexican border. See Sterling Publications Group Media Public Ltd. Co., "Global Hawk."

13. Grant, *Gulf War II*, 21.

14. Ibid.

15. Ibid., 22.

16. Some may argue that OIF disproves this trend. However, political fallout from OIF remains uncertain. It seems likely, however, that such large-scale actions will be the exception rather than the norm.

17. Keaney and Cohen, *Revolution in Warfare?* 213.

18. Clausewitz, *On War*, 69.

Chapter 3

Assessing the Air/Ground Relationship

The fact is that all the Services are now relying more on airpower and spending a greater [sic] share of their budgets on aerospace systems than at any time in history, whether they admit to an emerging predominant role for aerospace forces or not.

—Gene Myers

During the Iran War, my tank was my friend because I could sleep in it and know I was safe. . . . During this war my tank became my enemy . . . none of my troops would get near a tank at night because they just kept blowing up.

—Captured Iraqi officer, 1991

Republican Guard units outside of Baghdad are now dead. . . . We're not softening them up, we're killing them.

—Lt Gen T. Michael Moseley

Precision airpower has changed the face of modern combat and has become America's most useful military instrument. The first part of this chapter shows that the experience of recent conflicts indicates that land combat has been altered by precision airpower. At the heart of this proposition lies the notion that as long as America enjoys air superiority, enemies can no longer mass ground troops without facing certain destruction, as demonstrated in Desert Storm, Enduring Freedom, and Iraqi Freedom. Continuing improvements in all-weather PGM capability are working to deny the enemy the sanctuary of weather—a bitter reality discovered by Iraqi Republican Guard forces attempting to mass during a fierce desert sandstorm in 2003. Although airpower dramatically simplifies matters for US ground troops, it is not a panacea. Victory in both wars in Iraq required the combined forces of America's military. Nonetheless, airpower made the task immeasurably easier.

The second part of this chapter argues that airpower's inherent flexibility makes it the most politically useful form of force, allowing leaders to act with relatively little political risk. The extended air campaign at the start of Desert Storm and the choice to rely exclusively on airpower in Kosovo demonstrate that politicians will increasingly turn to airpower to mitigate the political risk associated with large-scale ground casualties.

Airpower, regardless of form or service, has become the favored instrument for military coercion, as operations against Libya, Iraq, Sudan, Afghanistan, and Serbia demonstrate. Operations Deny Flight and Northern and Southern Watch enabled the United States to deter unfriendly states at fractions of the costs normally associated with deployments of large numbers of ground forces. The chapter concludes with the proposition that due to its ability to change the modern battlefield and to provide real options for policy makers, airpower has become America's maneuver force of choice.[1]

Part 1: The Enemy Can No Longer Mass

Saddam Hussein was a formidable enemy in 1991. Iraq fielded one of the world's largest armies, operated a modern air force, and boasted an integrated air defense system (IADS) rivaled by few other nations. In spite of these strengths, Iraqi attempts to mass ground power against coalition forces consistently met with disaster. Battles at Al Khafji and infamous "highways of death" illustrated the perils of massing forces on the offense, while the air operations associated with the ground campaign wreaked havoc on forces attempting to concentrate defensively.

The Battle of Khafji was probably the most significant ground engagement of Desert Storm. In a series of encounters from 29 January to 1 February 1991, the Iraqi 3d Division attempted to lure American ground forces into combat by invading the Saudi border town of Al Khafji. As the attack developed, elements of two other Iraqi divisions massed and began to move south to reinforce the 3d Division. Orbiting JSTARS aircraft detected these movements and directed joint airpower to the scene.[2] Coalition airpower, including AC-130 gunships, Marine F/A-18s, and USAF A-10s, systematically dismantled the advancing force. Iraqi plans to continue reinforcing the invasion were "abandoned after suffering 2,000 casualties and having 300 of their vehicles destroyed mostly by air attacks."[3] The results of the slaughter were significant: Iraqi equipment losses were four times greater at Al Khafji than those suffered in the air war up to that point (table 2).[4] One captured Iraqi officer noted that "his brigade underwent more damage in thirty minutes than it had in the eight years in the previous war."[5]

Table 2. Iraqi equipment destroyed, 29 January–3 February 1991

	As of 29 January	As of 3 February
Tanks	80 (0)*	554 (177)
Armored Personnel Carriers	86 (3)	314 (81)
Artillery	308 (5)	425 (28)

Source: Eliot Cohen et al., *Gulf War Air Power Survey*, vol. 2, *Operations and Effects and Effectiveness* (Washington, DC: Government Printing Office, 1993), 240.

*Figures include Republican Guard losses, shown in parentheses.

Though few realized it at the time, Khafji was actually the climax of Iraqi operations. As Keaney and Cohen observed, "Subsequent to the experience at Al Khafji, the Iraqi army attempted no other attacks. They constructed more berms, dug deeper, dispersed supplies, changed to the use of smaller convoys in the Kuwaiti theater, moved headquarters' locations frequently, and increased the use of decoys in many areas."[6] More importantly the battle demonstrated that large-scale ground-force movements will almost certainly face devastation from precision airpower.

Throughout Desert Storm, Iraqi attempts at en masse movements most often met with utter destruction. Beginning on the evening of 25 February, coalition fixed-wing airpower destroyed more than 1,400 vehicles over a four-day period on the famous highway of death leading out of Kuwait City.[7] Further north, aircraft eliminated some 550–600 vehicles on the Hawr al Hammar causeway.[8] On 26 February, Army attack helicopters observed Iraqi troops and equipment fleeing north. In two separate engagements lasting little more than an hour, the helicopters destroyed 33 tanks, 22 armored personnel carriers, and 37 other vehicles.[9]

Few argue that Iraqi attempts to move in the open met with disaster, yet the fact that many of Saddam's forces survived to face US ground troops seems to suggest that the Iraqis were able to mass successfully in defensive positions. Actually the airpower decimated Saddam's entrenched ground forces and rendered the Iraqi army largely combat ineffective during the ground phase of the war.

Most of the contention over airpower in Desert Storm centers on what many call "the strategic air campaign."[10] This terminology conjures up images of attacks on Baghdad and obscures airpower's success in attacking Iraq's fielded forces before the start of the ground war. According to United States Central Command's (USCENTCOM) estimates, airpower destroyed 39 percent of Iraqi tanks, 32 percent of armored personnel carriers, and 47 percent of Iraqi artillery pieces during the strategic air campaign.[11]

Airpower took a greater toll on Iraqi military power than just the physical effects of bombs. The massed Iraqi defenses were "essentially paralyzed or demoralized," and those "left with a will to fight were able to do little more than face the attack and return fire, with no hope of maneuvering or being reinforced or achieving even tactical success."[12] Stephen Hosmer pointed out that of the approximately 400,000 Iraqi forces deployed in the Kuwaiti theater of operations (KTO), "no fewer than 160,000 (40 percent of those deployed) deserted" before the start of the ground war.[13] One Iraqi officer told his interrogators that he had surrendered because of B-52 strikes. When the interrogator pointed out that B-52s had not attacked the Iraqis' position, the soldier replied, "That is true, but I saw one that had been attacked."[14] In short, Iraqi attempts to mass forces in Desert Storm proved disastrous from both physical effects and psychological perspectives.

Loss of the ability to mass takes from an enemy far more than the ability to conduct successful military operations. Units that cannot mass also have difficulty training and obtaining supplies; they also become isolated by air attack. After the war one senior Iraqi officer reported that "after the start of Operation Desert Storm, he could no longer safely move his forces due to the threat of air attack. The air interdiction effort and degradation of the supply system stressed the Iraqi forces to and, in some cases, beyond the breaking point. Experienced armor officers were visibly shaken when they described helplessly watching the progressive destruction of their forces from the air."[15]

During the six-week air campaign before the beginning of the ground phase, coalition land forces intensified their training, continued to receive reinforcements, and solidified planning—all under the umbrella of air and space supremacy. More dramatically, air superiority allowed the coalition's combined force commander, Gen H. Norman Schwarzkopf, to reposition more than 270,000 troops hundreds of miles to the west without the Iraqis detecting the movement.[16] Air and space power effectively paralyzed, blinded, and progressively destroyed the Iraqis even before the ground war. As a result, the gap between Iraqi and coalition-force capabilities widened. Before coalition ground forces began to move into Iraq, the enemy was already in defeat. In spite of this unparalleled success, it is still clear that a ground war was necessary to actually eject the Iraqi army from Kuwait.

Coalition airpower made it possible for the ground campaign to succeed on an unprecedented scale. Advancing ground troops found a disheveled and broken Iraqi force. An Army combat engineer breaching the lines in Kuwait noted, "Aircraft had already destroyed most of their artillery. There was one unit still functioning when we came to the breach, delivering sporadic fire. They got swamped by our counterfire."[17] This soldier's experience was typical. There were few Iraqi units in Kuwait capable of serious resistance.

Some Iraqi forces did emerge from the burning desert at the Al Burgan oil fields to attack US marines who were advancing toward Kuwait City.[18] The Iraqis fought valiantly but in vain: "These guys mounting the counterattack just kept coming, even when our tanks and air just overwhelmed them."[19] This counterattack was the exception.

The most heavily engaged coalition units experienced steady but generally disorganized resistance. Brig Gen Carlton Fulford, USMC, relates, "Through the entire time, we were fighting tank units along the way. I wouldn't classify it as heavy: there were no heavy concentrations, but there were tank battles somewhere along my front almost always. . . . These tank battles were primarily one-on-one and we engaged them with TOW (tube launched, optically tracked, wire guided) missiles from Cobra helicopters and direct fire from our own tanks."[20]

The US Army's experiences were similar. The largest engagement of the ground war pitted five battalions of the US 1st Armored Division against the 2d Brigade of the Medina Armored Division and part of the Adnan Division (Republican Guard). The Battle of Medina Ridge, largely a surprise encounter, lasting about two hours, was characterized by the enemy's limited coordination and static defense. US ground forces, coupled with helicopter and fixed-wing CAS led to impressive results: over 300 enemy armored vehicles killed at the cost of only two friendlies and only one US soldier killed in action.[21]

Airpower critics cited the Republican Guard resistance at battles such as Medina Ridge and 73 Easting as proof that "good units can only be broken in direct combat."[22] General Schwarzkopf directed air planners to focus on the forward-regular Iraqi divisions rather than the Republican Guard behind them to soften up the enemy in areas of initial contact and thus reduce coalition ground-force casualties.[23]

Airpower resources are also finite, highlighting the importance of proper task prioritization. Airpower is rarely capable of eradicating an opposing ground force without assistance from the land component. It has been almost 80 years since an Airman of any importance has asserted anything to the contrary. In the aftermath of Desert Storm, it seems reasonable to claim that airpower can often greatly reduce the combat effectiveness of opposing ground forces, dramatically change the outcome of ground combat, and reduce friendly casualties.[24]

Limitations of Airpower in 1991

The successes of airpower in Desert Storm are remarkable. Despite the fact that the flat terrain of Iraq and Kuwait provided Airmen with near-optimal conditions for the employment of airpower, campaign planners faced several significant problems. Limited numbers of PGM-capable aircraft together with poor weather conditions and self-imposed altitude restrictions hampered airpower efforts against the Iraqi army. Although

Desert Storm will long be remembered for images of guided bombs falling precisely into ventilation shafts, the PGMs constituted only about 8 percent of total expenditures during the war. Of these, aircrews dropped only about one of every 40 precision munitions or 250 total tons of ordnance on the Iraqi army.[25] Therefore, 97 percent of munitions dropped on Iraq's fielded forces were so-called dumb bombs.

During the first Gulf War, weather conditions encountered were among the worst in the region in some 14 years.[26] All-weather precision bombs were unavailable in 1991. Strikes often had to be cancelled, or dumb bombs had to be dropped "through the weather," making the bombs even dumber. Rules of engagement also excluded bombing from low levels, thereby improving aircraft and aircrew survivability but magnifying the inaccuracy of dropping unguided munitions.

This combination of poor weather, few all-weather PGMs, and fairly high-bombing altitudes reduced airpower's effectiveness. The weather provided Iraqi forces with a form of sanctuary—albeit a tenuous one. The application of airpower was far from perfect in Desert Storm. The intervening decade would see airpower rapidly improve, and it would be tested again in the wake of 11 September 2001.

Operation Enduring Freedom—Afghanistan

In Operation Enduring Freedom 11 years later, Taliban forces in Afghanistan again proved that attempting to mass before US airpower is a fatal choice. Enduring Freedom will be discussed in detail in chapter 4 but bears mentioning here. In a recent account of the ground war in Afghanistan, Steven Biddle asserted that

> where the Taliban presented exposed or massed targets in the open, PGMs were extremely lethal. At Tarin Kowt on November 18, for example, Taliban forces tried to recapture the village by advancing in a column of vehicles up an exposed road. Frightened AMF [Afghan military forces] . . . defenders were prepared to abandon the village, but precision airstrikes called in by American commandos located on an overlooking ridgeline decimated the Taliban column, whose survivors fled the scene in disorder. Taliban reserves ordered forward to reinforce their defenses at Bai Beche were caught moving in the open . . . and were slaughtered by American airpower; officers who surveyed the scene afterward said it brought to mind the infamous "Highway of Death" leading out of Kuwait City in the 1991 Persian Gulf War.[27]

Taliban soldier Wahid Ahmed lamented, "We couldn't gather in large groups because that made us a target. We were waiting for our comrades to tell us what to do, but there was nothing to do but hide."[28] It is tempting to dismiss the success of airpower in Enduring Freedom because of the inferior nature of the Taliban forces, but the results were similar against a more formidable foe in America's second war with Iraq.

Operation Iraqi Freedom

Largely because of a lack of embedded-media reporting, airpower appeared less important to success in the second Gulf conflict. Despite the seeming absence of a preparatory air campaign in Iraqi Freedom, there had, in effect, been a "12 year strategic air campaign against Saddam Hussein."[29] In Southern and Northern Watch, Airmen repeatedly struck targets in Iraq in response to Hussein's aggression. Coalition aircraft dropped over 600 bombs in an operation known as Southern Focus that degraded Iraqi defenses prior to the Iraqi Freedom invasion.[30] Once the war began, Airmen demonstrated that air capabilities had improved dramatically since the first war with Saddam.

For the first time in the history of airpower, Airmen denied the enemy the luxury of a weather sanctuary.[31] On 25 March 2003, elements of three Republican Guard divisions moved south from Baghdad under a vicious sandstorm so severe that coalition ground forces had halted their advance to consolidate, refit, and refuel. The air component, however, was unrelenting. Drawing upon a full array of air and space sensors, air planners received a steady flow of data concerning the Iraqi troop movements.[32] The director of the air operations center (AOC) boasted that the coalition "knew the layout of the Republican Guard Forces better than their own division commanders did."[33] If the Iraqis repositioned in coherent formations, they were quickly targeted and engaged.[34] Coalition bombers attacked the Iraqis using the all-weather JDAMs and sometimes LGBs, nearly "obliterating Saddam's premier ground forces."[35]

Because airpower decimated the Iraqi force, its attack failed. The operation was not perfect, however. Frederick Kagan observed, "Although our airpower severely damaged the raiding forces and significantly reduced their combat power, the raiders nevertheless made contact with the lead elements of the 3d Infantry Division—which promptly destroyed them."[36] In spite of horrific weather conditions, airpower was able to degrade the enemy's combat power so that friendly ground forces were never seriously threatened. The all-weather JDAM proved its worth as Air Force aircraft went on to provide CAS even at the height of the storm.[37]

The nature of ground combat in Iraqi Freedom reflected the increasing maturity of coalition airpower since Desert Storm. Very large numbers of unguided bombs were dropped on Iraqi ground forces in 1991 while fully 56 percent were precision-guided bombs in 2003.[38] Coalition ground forces fought no armor battles at the battalion level or above. Most of the heavy fighting was with the fanatical Saddam Fedayeen militia who typically fielded only small arms and sport-utility vehicles. Defense analyst Anthony Cordesman noted, "There were strong indications that Iraqi forces had split up . . . and that the remaining elements of the Republican Guard were making major adjustments to defend Baghdad in small movements designed to minimize damage from the air."[39] A Republican Guard colonel admitted, "The divisions were essentially destroyed by airstrikes when they were still about 30 miles from their destination. . . . The Iraqi will to fight was broken outside Baghdad."[40] Many soldiers deserted their units out of fear of coalition air and ground power, and many others died in place. The commander of the 1st Brigade, 3d Infantry Division, US Army, observed, "We never really found any cohesive unit, of any brigade, of any Republican Guard Division."[41]

Summary

American air superiority means that enemies can no longer mass in meaningful numbers without fear of destruction.[42] In every instance since 1991 where the enemy has tried, the results have been catastrophic. Khafji and the highway of death in Desert Storm, Bai Beche in Enduring Freedom, and the sandstorm battle in Iraqi Freedom, all demonstrate that it is fatal for an enemy to concentrate his forces, even under the cover of severe weather. The Desert Storm battles of Medina Ridge and 73 Easting were likely the swan songs of heavy-armor engagements.

Part 2: Airpower, the American Way of War

The first part of this chapter focused on airpower's increasing effect on the outcome of land battle. Although this is highly visible and consumes much attention, it represents only part of the importance of airpower. Political considerations are equally important in determining the worth of a given military instrument. Weapons that are not or cannot be used are ineffective. Desert Storm, Enduring Freedom, and Iraqi Freedom all began in air campaigns for one simple reason. Since the days of Douhet, airpower has been seen as having the potential to make wars somehow shorter and cheaper.[43] In spite of its controversial record, this trait makes leaders willing to try airpower first.

Perhaps the clearest example of a political utility in airpower is the air war over Kosovo. Conditions in the Balkans deteriorated steadily in the 1990s until the international community could no longer turn a blind eye toward Serbia. As NATO pondered its options in the region, political factors predominated over military considerations.

Pres. William J. Clinton was facing impeachment, international tensions with Iraq were high, and there was little bipartisan support for a ground war in Europe in 1999. The administration faced a quandary: how to take action regarding Serbian "ethnic cleansing" in Kosovo without suffering undue political fallout. In a confusing attempt to clarify US policy, Secretary of State Madeline Albright asserted, "We are talking about using military force, but we are not talking about war. That is an important distinction."[44] The president assured the public that "I don't intend to put our troops in Kosovo to fight a war."[45] The administration also ruled out the use of ground forces in order to protect a delicate European consensus on the use of force.[46] Gen Wesley Clarke, commander of Supreme Allied Command Europe (SACEUR), pointed out at the time that "ground operations are inherently unpredictable and risk casualties among friendly forces."[47]

The United States, NATO, Commonwealth of Independent States (CIS), and the United Nations pursued several multilateral diplomatic initiatives with Serbia to no avail. The Clinton administration then decided that "execution of a phased air campaign was the best option for achieving [its] goals."[48] Caught on the horns of a largely political dilemma, NATO and the United States chose political flexibility over military efficacy.

Originally designed as a three-day air-coercion campaign, Allied Force burgeoned into an intense 78-day affair that seriously undermined NATO's credibility. Unfortunately NATO conducted the air campaign haphazardly. Lt Gen Michael C. Short, commander of Allied Air Forces Southern Europe, advocated conducting aggressive missions against Belgrade from the outset. However, political considerations resulted in a gradualist approach that evoked painful memories of the air war over Vietnam.

The specific reasons for Serbian submission to allied terms are unclear, but they certainly had little to do with Serbian losses suffered during the NATO counterland campaign. NATO had openly renounced a ground campaign, and Serb forces were free to disperse, surviving the war nearly unscathed. Evidence suggests that total Serb army losses numbered fewer than nine tanks, 20 armored personnel carriers, and 30 artillery pieces.[49]

Analysts disagree on the results of NATO's campaign against Serbia. One noted academic went so far as to claim, "Now there is a new date to fix on the calendar: June 3, 1999, when the capitulation of President Milosevic proved that a war can be won by airpower alone," while some ascribed NATO's success to other political factors.[50] The real lesson of Allied Force is that precision airpower is no panacea. Poor weather, unprecedented political constraints, and Serbian tactics ruined the air campaign. But it was the lack of a credible ground campaign that degraded counterland air operations most. General Short stated, "Airpower is clearly much more effective if we have an army in the field to fix the enemy army and make him move and make him predictable."[51] Indeed NATO's greatest successes likely came when the Kosovo Liberation Army (KLA) launched an offensive forcing the Serb army to mass.[52] It might have been that a serious NATO ground threat would have enhanced the utility of airpower, shortened the war, and perhaps saved many lives in the process.

Coercion

Thanks to its precision, national leaders can use airpower as coercion, knowing that missiles and bombs will very likely hit their targets and reduce the risk of collateral damage—and associated political fallout. The compelling quality of precision airpower is that it provides alternatives to all-or-nothing military commitment. America's reprisal raid in Lebanon (1982), the attack on Libya (1986), Deliberate Force (1995), and Desert Fox (1998), were all exclusively airpower actions. In each case the United States successfully demonstrated political resolve without widening the conflict or jeopardizing large numbers of American ground troops—results that could not be achieved except through airpower.

Political leaders will increasingly choose those options that produce the least political risk. In 1992 former Pres. George H. W. Bush demonstrated this phenomenon by ordering attacks against Iraq's Zafraniyah nuclear fabrication facility only 13 miles from the center of Baghdad. His press secretary explained at the time, "We wanted to use the missiles because it did not put US personnel in jeopardy. We did not have to suffer the risk of having personnel go down."[53] President Clinton, who was particularly attuned to public opinion, used cruise missiles on at least seven occasions between 1993 and 1998 to carry out American policy.[54]

Clearly airpower's flexibility and political utility make it an attractive choice for US leaders considering military coercion. Airpower's capabilities are not strictly limited to actual force application. The threat of airpower can be a powerful motivator for potential enemies and can serve a vital role in deterring America's foes.

Deterrence

Airpower plays a vital, if underappreciated, role in "deterring" America's enemies. Operation Provide Comfort (later known as Northern Watch) provided safe haven for Iraq's Kurdish population for nearly 12 years. The Kurds lived in relative peace inside Saddam's Iraq under the protective umbrella of coalition airpower establishing an economy, schools, and even a degree of autonomy. Southern Watch safeguarded the borders of Kuwait and Saudi Arabia while providing valuable ISR and responsive strike options for the coalition. NATO deterred Serbian aggression in the Balkans with Deny Flight.[55] This highly successful operation prevented warring parties from using airpower to intensify their conflicts and made an important contribution to the Balkan peace process.[56]

These deployments constituted America's longest sustained military operation since Vietnam, and "air policing" operations allowed the United States to achieve major strategic goals at relatively low costs.[57] To be sure, ground forces remain an indispensable element, and they were deployed frequently to the Persian Gulf during the 1990s in support of airpower and diplomacy. It was the continuous air presence, however, that was the primary deterrence to Iraqi aggression while guaranteeing that the coalition would have time to deploy additional air and ground forces, if need be. Airpower was the cornerstone of America's deterrence policies in the 1990s. Col Paul White noted in 2001 that "the [Iraqi no-fly] zones . . . exerted a constant, credible military threat against Saddam. The risk of retaliation by airstrikes has been crucial in preventing Saddam from threatening his neighbors."[58]

Over the last two decades, airpower has become the American way of war. Its precision and flexibility enable political leaders to effectively execute American national policy. Critics admonish leaders that the PGMs are no substitute for strategy. In the end Clausewitz is right—war and politics *are* inseparable. Because airpower offers leaders options with reduced political risk, it will continue to be the instrument of choice in matters of coercion, deterrence, and war.

Conclusion

Events throughout the 1990s showed that airpower has changed the paradigm of modern conventional combat. Where America enjoys air superiority, her enemies can no longer mass against friendly forces without fear of annihilation from the air. Iraqi attempts to concentrate at Khafji led to utter devastation, dug-in forces died in dramatic fashion in Kuwait, and the Taliban were summarily destroyed each time their soldiers "presented exposed or massed targets in the open."[59] Improvements in ISR and all-weather precision capability have eliminated the sanctuary of weather, as demonstrated by the ill-fated Iraqi sandstorm attacks in 2003.

The inability to mass signals a historic change in the conduct of warfare. A force that cannot mass is incapable of carrying out large-scale conventional operations. As a result, enemies will increasingly disperse, conceal, and resort to tactics of the weak, such as guerrilla warfare, insurgency, and terrorism.[60]

This has meaning for air and ground power alike. To the Airman, it means that enemies of the future will work harder to avoid detection. For ground forces the implications are much more dramatic. US ground troops are still generally trained and equipped to fight a peer enemy using symmetrical strategies. If the enemy is incapable of massing, it does not make sense to have a force designed primarily to fight a massed-enemy ground force. The American military must reform its organization, structure, and strategy to adapt to the changing circumstances of modern war. These are the themes discussed in the last chapter.

Finally, air campaigns in Desert Storm, Enduring Freedom, Iraqi Freedom, and especially the air war over Kosovo show that airpower is the American way of war. Kosovo also offers a glimpse of the future. Airpower struggled in that conflict because there was no accompanying friendly ground force. This is not to say that all campaigns must be massive affairs like Desert Storm; rather, "the ground force . . . needs to present a credible one-dimensional ground threat to the opposing force."[61] A "credible threat," however, "does not mean that the United States must attain a numerical advantage on the ground, or even numerical parity."[62] Operations in Afghanistan seem to demonstrate this. In Enduring Freedom, small numbers of ground troops were able to leverage airpower to create effects on the battlefield disproportionate to their size. That idea will be explored more in the next chapter.

Notes

1. Definition derived from Givens, *Turning the Vertical Flank*, 15.
2. Coalition air response to this attack was initially sluggish. US Marines provided initial reports of the Iraqi attack. The JSTARS detected the reinforcing divisions.
3. W. Gordon and Trainor, *Generals' War*, 287.
4. Cohen et al., *Gulf War Air Power Survey*, vol. 2, 240.
5. Keaney and Cohen, *Revolution in Warfare?* 95.

6. Ibid., 96.

7. Ibid., 99. Of these vehicles, most were stolen Kuwaiti vehicles. Only about 28 of the vehicles were armored.

8. Ibid. Of these vehicles, only 10–20 were armored vehicles.

9. Scales, *Certain Victory*, 290. Scales asserts that the Army could have done much more substantial damage had it not been for Air Force fire-coordination procedures. Benjamin Lambeth takes issue with this claim. Lambeth, *Transformation of American Air Power*, n.p.

10. Desert Storm continues to be seen in chronological phases by many as a strategic air campaign followed by an Army ground campaign with air-power support. In reality, only about 15 percent of air strikes were flown against "strategic" target sets, compared to 56 percent against Iraqi ground forces. Keaney and Cohen, *Revolution in Warfare?* 55. John Andreas Olsen asserts that the percentage of strikes against true strategic targets was closer to 2 percent of the overall effort. See Olsen, *Strategic Air Power*, 265.

11. Keaney and Cohen assert that although the estimate of the actual numbers of equipment destroyed before the ground war was inaccurate, the percentages were sound. See Keaney and Cohen, *Revolution in Warfare?* 108–10. Keaney and Cohen found USCENTCOM data in US DOD, *Conduct of the Persian Gulf War*, 254.

12. Keaney and Cohen, *Revolution in Warfare?* 101.

13. Hosmer, *Psychological Effects*, 153.

14. Ibid., 165.

15. US DOD, *Conduct of the Persian Gulf War*, 214.

16. Ibid., 245. This movement was larger in scope than Gen George Patton's famous movement to attack the German flank at the Battle of the Bulge.

17. Bin, Hill, and Jones, *Desert Storm*, 175.

18. See W. Gordon and Trainor, *Generals' War*, 363–69, for an account of the Al Burqan oil-field fight.

19. Bin, Hill, and Jones, *Desert Storm*, 183.

20. Ibid., 186.

21. For an in-depth discussion, see Scales, *Certain Victory*, 292–300; and ibid., 193.

22. Scales, *Certain Victory*, 368.

23. US DOD, *Conduct of the Persian Gulf War*, 213.

24. General Scales admitted, "Iraqi losses from the air may never be truly known but, while less than the Combatant Commander's 50 percent objective, were sufficient to demoralize and disrupt all but the best of the Iraqi ground forces." Scales, *Certain Victory*, 368.

25. US Government Accounting Office, *Operation Desert Storm*, 218.

26. US DOD, *Conduct of the Persian Gulf War*, 227.

27. Biddle, "Afghanistan and the Future of Warfare," 34.

28. Haag, "OIF Veterans Discuss Lessons."

29. Briefing, Deptula. See also Murray and Scales, *Iraq War*, 183.

30. M. Gordon, "US Air Raids," cited in Grant, *Gulf War II*, 3.

31. It could be argued that Allied Force and the debut of the B-2/JDAM combination represent this turning point. However, these sorties represented a small percentage of the total effort and had no meaningful impact on the enemy's ability to use weather as a shield.

32. Grant, *Gulf War II*, 21.

33. Graham and Loeb, "Air War of Might, Coordination, and Risks."

34. Ibid.

35. Grant, *Gulf War II*, 21.

36. Kagan, "War and Aftermath," 3–27.

37. Pirnie to the author, letter. See also After-Action Report, "3rd Infantry Division."

38. Conetta, "Catastrophic Interdiction," 3.

39. Cordesman, *Iraq War*, 109.

40. Briefing, Deptula, slide 8.

41. Ibid.

42. Pirnie et al., *Beyond Close Air Support*, 89.

43. Operation Southern Focus was essentially an undeclared air campaign designed to "soften up" Iraqi defenses in preparation for broader military action.

44. Correll, *Strategy, Requirements and Forces*, 14.

45. Cited in Lambeth, *NATO's Air War for Kosovo*, 19.

46. Rostker, "Transformation," 139.

47. Ibid.

48. Cordesman, *Lessons and Non-Lessons*, 19.

49. Nardulli et al., *Disjointed War*, 55.

50. Keegan, cited in Hinen, "Kosovo," 1.

51. Blechman and Lum, "Rethinking Transformation," 38–42.

52. In the aftermath of the war, NATO and US sources claimed that bombers struck some 800–1,200 Serb forces caught in the open as a result of the Kosovo Liberation Army advance, killing as many as 200. Controversy surrounds this claim. See Cordesman, *Lessons and Non-Lessons*, 255; and Priest, "Decisive Battle."

53. Rip and Hasik, *Precision Revolution*, 363.

54. Ibid., 362.

55. Nordeen, *Air Warfare in the Missile Age*, 241.

56. "Operation Deny Flight lasted from 12 April 1993 to 20 December 1995, when the International Implementation Force assumed responsibilities for the implementation of the military aspects of the Peace Agreement on Bosnia-Herzegovina." Headquarters Allied Forces Southern Command, "AFSOUTH Fact Sheet." For details of Serb aggression, see Nordeen, *Air Warfare in the Missile Age*, 241.

57. White, "Airpower and a Decade of Containment," 35–39.

58. Ibid.

59. Biddle, "Afghanistan and the Future of Warfare," 34.

60. See Arquilla and Ronfeldt, *Swarming*. Another potential tactic aimed at solving this dilemma is "swarming," which may be defined as "engaging an adversary from all directions simultaneously" (vii). Chechens frequently used

swarming tactics against the Russians, attacking in small bands of 12–20 fighters that would "pulse" to the attack and then dissipate. If a well-armed, properly organized force with superior information is able to transition rapidly from complete concealment to massed formations, it could present a difficult problem for airpower. However, the argument offered here remains valid: where the enemy masses in the open, he is most vulnerable to airpower. In order to defeat swarming, airpower must continue to improve its ability to persist over the battlefield. The Serb army in Kosovo, al-Qaeda in the Shah-e-Khot Valley, and the continuing insurgency in Iraq likely tell us more about future combat than Desert Storm or Iraqi Freedom.

61. Mason, "New American Way of War?" 13.

62. Ibid.

Chapter 4

The Afghan Model and Beyond

The conflict in Afghanistan has taught the United States more about the future of our military than a decade of blue ribbon panels and think-tank symposiums.

—Pres. George W. Bush

Let me make sure I'm clear. Airpower will make a differ-ence and if the enemy outsmarts precise weapons you can bet there will be a smart American guy on the ground and in the air who would use airpower to hit him from another angle, then another, then another.

—SSgt Gabe Brown,
USAF Combat Controller

America launched Operation Enduring Freedom on 7 October 2001 to crush the al-Qaeda terror network and remove the un-palatable Taliban regime that sheltered it. The campaign in Af-ghanistan is significant for many reasons, but perhaps the most enduring lesson is the value of airpower. Previous chapters have shown that airpower's lethality and political utility have combined to make airpower the most useful military tool in America's arse-nal—a fact dramatically underscored during Enduring Freedom. A handful of SOFs working closely with indigenous rebel forces har-nessed precision airpower to topple the Taliban regime. To be sure, the Taliban fielded a fourth-rate military force. But Afghanistan has long been a bane for invading armies—Alexander the Great struggled there, and attempts by the British, Russian, and Soviet empires to subdue the Afghans failed miserably. This legacy led Milton Bearden to dub Afghanistan "the Graveyard of Empires," and in the fall of 2001, it seemed reasonable to think that the United States would fare no better.[1] Instead, indigenous allies, highly trained SOF personnel, and, most importantly, airpower were able to accomplish their objectives quickly and with small loss of life.

While the campaign against the Taliban began with moral clarity, military options in Afghanistan were very limited. The daunting logistical and operational challenges that accompany operations in Afghanistan had scarcely changed in the centuries since Genghis Khan first transited the Khyber Pass. The extreme geography of Afghanistan and a lack of nearby basing possibilities led USCENTCOM to officially predict that it would take "months" to prepare for a major military operation in Afghanistan.[2] This estimate was predicated on an orthodox view of warfare and operations by heavy ground forces. As the American public grew more anxious for a decisive response to the events of 11 September 2001 (9/11), the administration searched for options, ultimately settling on a combination of SOFs, proxy forces, and airpower.[3] This became known as the "Afghan model," and it was extremely successful.[4] This force combination was originally intended only to prepare the battlefield for "decisive operations" by conventional Army troops—not to win outright.[5] Friendly land forces, relying heavily on airpower, were able to lay siege to the enemy capital less than five weeks after the start of the campaign and well before the introduction of significant numbers of US ground forces. The coalition installed a friendly regime in Afghanistan barely two months into the conflict and thereby dramatically reduced al-Qaeda's ability to threaten the world.[6]

This chapter seeks to expand discussion of the Afghan model to argue that it represents a highly successful war-fighting tool made possible by precision airpower and that experiences in Afghanistan were not anomalous. While the combination of SOFs and airpower is hardly new, precision airpower has changed the military equation dramatically. Airpower enabled the United States and its allies to prevail against better-armed and better-trained Taliban that outnumbered friendly ground forces by a ratio of nearly three to one.

Part 1: Origins of the Afghan Model

SOF personnel have long relied on airpower for transportation and CAS, because special forces (SF) "A" teams are required to travel light, and they came to rely on CAS in order to compensate for a lack of armor and artillery.[7] As early as 1961, US air commandos directed T-28 and B-26 aircraft in Operation Farm Gate to provide CAS and interdiction missions in support of America's South Vietnamese allies.[8] Later, Operations Shining Brass and Prairie Fire featured SOF teams infiltrating Laos to coordinate airpower against the clandestine traffic on the Ho Chi Minh Trail.[9]

Between Vietnam and Desert Storm, the relationship between SOFs and airpower remained fairly static. Since Desert Storm, advancing technology significantly enhanced SOF's capabilities and began to change the relationship between airpower and SOFs. Portable laser designators now enable teams to direct laser-guided weapons dropped from aircraft overhead. The GPS enhances overland navigation and allows teams to pass precise targeting data to orbiting aircraft.

A Marriage of Convenience

The president was under intense pressure to avenge the bloodiest attack on American soil since Pearl Harbor.[10] Regardless of any military considerations, the public wanted revenge. At the same time, the rest of the world community urged the president to limit retaliation to those directly responsible for the attack on America, so he needed to tread very carefully.[11] The DOD is alleged to have placed "force caps" on the services—restrictions on the total number of personnel involved in Afghanistan—to avoid the appearance of "going to war" against Islam.[12]

Uzbekistan, Tajikistan, Turkmenistan, and Pakistan are ideally situated geographically for staging military operations in Afghanistan, but the United States lacked the especially friendly relationships with these nations that would have allowed rapid deployment of US forces to Central Asia.[13] Overcoming these diplomatic challenges required delicate negotiation—a very time-consuming process. Therefore, in the immediate term at least, only small numbers of SOFs would be available for a US military force inside Afghanistan.

As one Army planner commented, Afghanistan is "the most strategically impossible place to introduce force on the entire . . . planet."[14] Large deployment of US force depends on seaports and railheads—neither of which is readily available in or around Afghanistan. Moving troop concentrations and their equipment by air is a time-consuming process and requires a substantial airhead that was also lacking. The net result of these long distances was that quick projection of US land power to the region proved impossible.[15]

Despite these challenges, the United States had one important factor in its favor in Enduring Freedom—a considerable proxy force on the ground. Over nearly a decade of fighting the Taliban, the Afghan Northern Alliance (NA) had grown to a force some 15,000 strong.[16] In spite of inferior numbers, these rebels had managed to stalemate the Taliban in the outlying provinces of northern Afghanistan. However, being led by warlords who often financed their operations through opium sales, the NA was politically unattractive.

Political pressures and the limited options available to the United States led to a shotgun wedding between SOFs, airpower, and the NA at the beginning of Enduring Freedom. As General Short said, "It was something we just stumbled upon. If it had been up to [the] United States . . . under different circumstances, we probably never would have come up with it."[17] In spite of the haphazard nature of its conception, the notion of combining SOFs, proxy forces, and airpower on the modern battlefield would prove its worth.

The New Model Goes to War

Even projecting combat airpower presented a challenge; carrier aircraft would fly over 700 miles one way to attack the Taliban, bombers based in the Indian Ocean faced a 5,000-mile round-trip, and land-based fighters flew sorties as long as 15 hours from Kuwait.[18] The early air attacks were largely ineffective. The traditional "strategic" air campaign conducted by the United States suffered from a lack of leadership and infrastructure targets in Afghanistan. As a result, operations quickly depleted fixed-target lists, and the ground situation changed very little after nearly a month of bombing. The American public began to grow restless, and the term *stalemate* started to surface in media accounts of the war. Peter Beaumont's report in the *Observer* that "the war had become bogged down" typified press reports of the period.[19]

By the time US SOFs began to support the NA's Gen Abdul Rashid Dostum, American airpower had been pummeling the Taliban for two weeks. Then on 19 October 2001, with the air war stagnating and political pressure for results mounting,

Secretary of Defense Donald Rumsfeld announced that US troops would provide direct assistance to Afghan opposition groups.[20] Two days later, SOF personnel called in their first air strikes in support of the NA advance toward Mazar-e-Sharif.[21]

The addition of SOF-directed precision airpower completely overwhelmed Taliban forces. Major combat actions using the new model began when Dostum's forces conquered the village of Bishqab. By the end of October, 80 percent of the air effort was dedicated to CAS, and the administration publicly acknowledged that SOF personnel were working directly in support of the NA.[22] A rapid succession of victories followed in November: Bai Beche fell on the fifth, Mazar-e-Sharif on the 10th, Kabul on the 13th, and Konduz on the 26th. In dramatic fashion, airpower enabled the NA to gain control of nearly half the country between the ninth and 12th of November. On 6 December—just 60 days after the start of the war—Mullah Omar and senior Taliban officials abandoned Kandahar and went into hiding, effectively ending Taliban rule in Afghanistan.[23]

The air campaign in Afghanistan stood traditional war-fighting doctrine on its head. Standard military doctrine maintained that success against an organized defense normally requires a three-to-one offensive advantage. Enduring Freedom demonstrated that this rule of thumb is not necessarily valid when precision airpower is available. Taliban forces outnumbered the NA throughout the campaign, often in ratios of "thousands to hundreds."[24] At Mazar-e-Sharif, for example, over 5,000 Taliban troops defended the city against some 2,000 NA soldiers.[25] In addition to superior numbers and better-trained troops, the Taliban also enjoyed superior firepower, including Soviet artillery and some 450 pieces of armor (including main battle tanks) left over from the Soviet occupation.[26] In contrast, NA forces relied almost completely on small arms and traveled largely on foot or horseback.

The campaign against Mazar-e-Sharif had been ineffective in the opening days of Enduring Freedom largely due to these NA disadvantages. In early November, airpower began to focus on Taliban defenses in the Mazar-e-Sharif area, and the initiative shifted to the rebels. One by one the cities surrounding Mazar-e-Sharif fell to the NA. Throughout, the NA fought bravely, spearheading its attacks on enemy armor with some 1,000 lightly armed fighters on horseback. Airpower rather than cavalry, however, turned the tide; and in the final assault, the NA killed hundreds of Taliban soldiers, capturing some 3,000 others.[27] More importantly the seizure of Mazar-e-Sharif opened a vital land bridge with Uzbekistan, enabling the United States to expand its logistical base for operations in Afghanistan.

Coalition airpower transformed the NA into an extraordinarily lethal fighting force. As one warlord noted, "Tiger 01 has killed more Taliban in 48 hours with CAS than the NA has been able to kill in the previous year."[28] Air Force combat controllers, working closely with Army SFs and NA commanders, relentlessly applied airpower to enemy positions and systematically dismantled the Taliban from the air. Intense combat on the ground was the exception rather than the rule when airpower was available.

There were few US conventional forces in Afghanistan when the Taliban fell. The majority of those forces were providing security at various bases in the country rather than engaging in combat against the Taliban.[29] For the first time in history, the combination of small numbers of SOFs and airpower served as the focal point of a major conventional land campaign. The synergy created by SOFs, the NA, and coalition airpower reversed nearly a decade of Taliban dominance in Afghanistan in a matter of weeks. Nevertheless, many criticize the Afghan model as a suitable paradigm for future operations.

Part 2: Criticism of the New Model

In retrospect, military victory in Afghanistan seemed easy. Since the fall of the Taliban, academics and politicians alike have maintained that the Afghan model was not easily repeatable, suggesting that it could succeed only if the circumstances found in Enduring Freedom were exactly replicated. Secretary of State Colin Powell, speaking in December 2001, warned that the model would not work in Iraq: "They're two different countries with two different regimes, two different military capabilities. . . . They are so significantly different that you can't take the Afghan model and immediately apply it to Iraq."[30] Dr. Milan Vego, writing in July of 2002, asserted, "In short, the use of airpower in combination with SF on the ground can be expected to be successful in some counterterrorist operation or campaign in the future, but not in major regional contingencies."[31] Events in Iraq would prove both wrong.

As in 2001 it was only when political circumstances prevented large-scale deployment of land power that planners turned to airpower. The original war plan for Iraqi Freedom called for the Army's 4th Infantry Division to deploy in northern Iraq—an option denied by Turkey's refusal to grant staging rights to American ground forces. Instead, SFs and airpower replaced an entire infantry division. Fifty SOF A teams infiltrated northern Iraq with orders to combine forces with the local Kurdish *peshmerga* ("those who face death"). Using airpower as their main striking force, the combined forces commander (CFC) assigned these fighters three primary missions:

1. Harass the 13 Iraqi divisions on the "Green Line," preventing their redeployment to oppose coalition forces advancing on Baghdad from the south.

2. Destroy camps in northern Iraq belonging to the Ansar al-Islam terrorist group.

3. Use SOFs to capture key oil fields near Kirkuk and stabilize the northern cities of Mosul and Kirkuk.[32]

The *peshmerga* consisted of some 50,000–70,000 militia troops stationed throughout northern Iraq.[33] Clearly, the Iraqis outnumbered the Kurds, but reliable estimates of the ratio during the war are unavailable. Often, the number of *peshmerga* who reported for battle varied widely from the numbers promised by militia leaders.[34] As a fighting force, the Kurds' offensive skills were "nonexistent," often consisting of direct frontal assaults against superior firepower. On the defense, the Kurdish militia was "acceptable" due to "plenty of practice digging in and establishing a defense after years of anticipating an Iraqi attack."[35] Iraqi forces possessed armor and artillery, which made the lightly armed Kurds extremely vulnerable without air support. Capt Joe Swiecki, who commanded an A team during Iraqi Freedom, asserted that Kurdish "skill was comparable and their motivation was higher than the Iraqis. . . . With air support, the Kurds were able to overcome their lack of armor and indirect support. . . . It was air power that allowed the Kurds to overcome their lack of equipment."[36]

Many details of the operation remain classified, but the experiences of Operational Detachment A (ODA) Teams 063 and 065 illustrate the potential of the SOFs/*peshmerga*/airpower combination. Augmented with highly skilled Air Force combat controllers and reinforced by as many as 100 *peshmerga*, these units engaged in almost continuous combat from 24 March until 10 April 2003.[37] Engagements varied in intensity, but occasionally the Iraqis applied determined resistance. Air Force combat controllers directed CAS on all but two of those days in the case of ODA 065 and in 11 out of 16 of ODA 063's engagements.[38] In contrast to the Taliban, Iraqi defenders fought bravely, and *peshmerga* success against them was often far from assured. On 3 April, for example, Capt Eric Carver led his team in a tenacious fight:

> Advanced with local *peshmerga* forces 8 km [kilometer] into enemy division area with one battalion of Saddam Fedayeen and one battalion Republican Guard. Engaged in heavy ground combat . . . with enemy battalion sized element supported by 120 mm [millimeter], 82 mm, 60 mm mortars and heavy machine guns and various small arms. Enemy forces tried to launch a counter-attack; members of the team were in direct combat with the enemy. Enemy attack in the morning was fought off with small arms and close air support. Enemy reorganized and mounted another battalion sized attack in the afternoon again. ODA and *peshmerga* forces fought off attack with crew served weapons and small arms. The element was in the process of being flanked when close air support of bombers and strafing runs by F-14s forced the enemy to withdraw to original positions.[39]

Often *peshmerga* faced a well-motivated Iraqi enemy that was more numerous and better armed.[40] American airpower enabled an outnumbered Kurdish force to remain in contact with and inflict serious punishment on the enemy. After several days of suffering coalition air attacks, Iraqi forces retreated, and ODA 065 and its *peshmerga* continued their advance on the city of Mosul. Anecdotes like this one were familiar throughout northern Iraq. SF teams routinely accepted a two-to-one numerical disadvantage when they knew airpower was available. The commander of ODA 063 observed, "The Kurds were willing to do anything we asked as long as we guaranteed air support."[41]

The battle of Debecka Pass demonstrated that the model is not risk free. Two SOF teams confronted an entire Iraqi motorized rifle company, including multiple tanks and armored vehicles. Enemy artillery fire was intense, and, as in the case of ODA 065, the battle was a close-run event. Unfortunately on the first day of the battle, airpower ultimately "did more harm than good," as an F-14 mistakenly bombed the wrong position, killing 17 Kurds and wounding 40 others.[42] Low cloud ceilings, lack of precision ordnance, and protective (close enfilade) placement of Iraqi armor combined to present a challenging target for airpower.[43] After a fierce four-and-one-half-hour firefight, courageous American resistance and expert employment of Javelin antitank missiles repelled the Iraqis.[44] The next day the team fared better: the Iraqis mounted a sizable counterattack, but CAS arrived in a timely manner. This time the Iraqis retreated "after the first couple of bombs went off."[45] As one SF team leader related, "In my opinion, we (SF) could not have won the northern front without air. Armor or Mechanized Infantry forces could have crushed the Northern Iraqi forces, probably faster than we did it; however, the cost would have been significantly more American lives (we lost none). The combination of airpower, SOFs, and Kurdish *peshmerga* allowed the United States to focus ground forces elsewhere, and preserve combat power and American lives."[46]

In Afghanistan and Iraq, the new model helped America overcome political and geographical obstacles to produce victory in situations where the normal forms of force application were impossible. In retrospect, arguments that the model is not repeatable were obviously wrong. The new model has quickly become a valuable tool in America's arsenal and has important ramifications for future conflicts. As with any war-fighting doctrine, it is not universally applicable nor is it without limitations.

Indigenous Allies

Steven Biddle contended that the tactical qualities of the proxy force are critical: "Even with precision air support, indigenous allies need a combination of skill, motivation and equipment at least broadly *comparable to their enemy's* to prevail" (emphasis added).[47] Airpower obviously cannot transform an unruly mob into a fighting force that is up to American military standards, but Biddle's assertion about indigenous allies is only partially correct. The skill of the proxy fighting force is important, but it is their skill and motivation *in relation to the plan of operations* that matters most—*not skill in relation to that of the enemy.* In the two most well-known battles where many believe the Afghan allies fought poorly, misunderstanding of Afghan motivations and lack of sound American planning most directly affected the outcomes.

Intelligence placed bin Laden in Tora Bora, and Afghan fighters, expected to execute the majority of the attack plan at Tora Bora, found themselves in a difficult operation for which they were ill prepared and unmotivated.[48] The plan consisted of two basic elements: (1) airpower was to pummel the cave complexes in hopes of dislodging the enemy, and (2) thousands of Afghans would exploit the results of the bombing by fighting cave-to-cave and by providing a "backstop" to prevent the enemy from fleeing to Pakistan.[49] Conditions at Tora Bora were exceptionally difficult: most fighting took place above 10,000 feet—one Army advisor reported, "You have to see it to believe it. I personally conducted a recon up to 9,000 ft. and I was still in the foothills. Steep peaks, deep valleys, small foot trails, and that was the good part."[50] Taliban and al-Qaeda fighters had fortified already-favorable defensive positions and had stockpiled supplies and ammunition. As Richard Stewart observed, "With large numbers of well-supplied, fanatical al-Qaeda troops dug into extensive fortified positions, Tora Bora appeared to be an extremely tough target."[51]

The force chosen to execute this difficult operation was ill prepared for the task. One Afghan leader noted, "When we started off in Tora Bora, we didn't have enough real information . . . but the Americans were in a big hurry to start the offensive. We had a force there, but we didn't have a good enough intelligence network."[52] Fighters arrived at Tora Bora with little preparation or inadequate equipment. As one Afghan leader recalled, "I only heard about the offensive that day at 7 a.m. . . . My father told me, 'just go,' so I . . . took 700 soldiers. We got there, but I don't know for what. We had no food or anything."[53] In many cases, these troops allegedly accepted bribes from al-Qaeda fighters in return for safe passage.[54] One man admitted that he had taken "20 important Arabs into Pakistan."[55]

The results of the operation at Tora Bora were predictable: "A few al-Qaeda were captured, but most of them fought to the death or slipped away into nearby Pakistan. The whereabouts of Osama bin Laden, or even whether he had been in the Tora

Bora region in the first place remained a mystery."[56] In the aftermath of this failure, most criticism focused on the skill of the indigenous allies. A British Special Air Services (SAS) officer described a common view of the outcome: "The idea was for native troops to provide a blocking force who were simply not up to the task."[57] Most accounts focused on the tactical skill of the Afghans, failing to adequately consider the difficulty of the mission and an even more important factor—their motivation.

Understanding the motivation of the indigenous ally is a critical consideration in proxy warfare. Most Afghans were unaware of the attacks of 9/11, and the thought of America under attack was not a powerful motivator for them. The Afghans had little quarrel with al-Qaeda—their enemy was the Taliban. Once the Taliban fell, the meaning of the war changed for the rebels. As a RAND analyst observed, "The Afghans didn't have much enthusiasm for fighting al-Qaeda in the post-Taliban era."[58] Local commanders, accustomed to years of factional infighting, were reportedly "reluctant" to pursue the enemy into the White Mountains, "preferring instead to stay in newly liberated Jalalabad to stake out their own turf."[59] A key Army SF advisor to the Afghans confirmed, "On numerous occasions, I had to personally sit down and negotiate with [Afghan] General Hazrat Ali and convince him to stay in the fight."[60]

To strengthen Afghan commitment at Tora Bora, American officials paid the warlords cash bonuses, ranging from $30,000 for supplies to perhaps as much as "several hundred thousand dollars" in return for their support.[61] The drawback to relying on financial incentives, though, was that the local allies were not deeply committed to the cause. As a result, "their interests clearly diverged from those of the United States . . . when it came to hunting down al Qaeda holdouts who were dug in and determined to fight to the finish."[62]

Motivation is a critical factor in war, and it becomes more important as combat conditions grow more dangerous. Afghan commanders had very good reasons for wanting to avoid Tora Bora. They had successfully held off the Soviets in that area and had an intimate understanding of the difficulties inherent in fighting in the White Mountains. The operation was sufficiently challenging that even US Marines refused the opportunity to commit forces there.[63] At Tora Bora, extreme altitudes and "unbelievable" terrain led to conditions that completely favored the enemy. Assertions that "bombing without energetic ground exploitation" led to al-Qaeda's escape at Tora Bora simply ignore the enormity of the task.[64] According to Col Mark Rosengard, USA, director of operations for Task Force (TF) Dagger, "You can't find the infantry organization in anybody's army that can occupy and control Tora Bora."[65]

Operations at Tora Bora were difficult, dangerous, and most importantly, part of America's war, not the Afghans' war. As the mayor of Jalalabad, a veteran *mujaheddeen*, noted, "They are just doing these things for the money. . . . One American came to meet me, and he was very angry. . . . He said he was angry because they spent so much money here and too many Arabs escaped. He asked my opinion about this, and I got angry. I said that they put all this money in the pockets of commanders who did not organize anything. In a war, you need strategy. They were moving here, going there, coming back at night—it wasn't a real war."[66]

Many pundits blamed the use of the Afghan military forces for the United States' failure to capture or kill bin Laden at Tora Bora.[67] With a better understanding of proxy-force motivations and an appreciation for the difficulty of the task, it seems clear, now, that hopes for dramatic success at Tora Bora were overly optimistic. To expect a poorly trained ally to execute a strategy that would be difficult for even highly trained troops is unreasonable, and the results were, likewise, predictable.

Anaconda and the Need for Thorough Planning

US forces planned to use Afghan fighters differently in Operation Anaconda. This time the Afghans were to be the "hammer" in a hammer-and-anvil maneuver. The Afghans would undertake the difficult task of dislodging the enemy from villages at the base of the Shah-e-Khot Valley and drive them against an American "anvil." Unfortunately, "feeling rushed into the fight, finding themselves under heavy enemy fire and suffering casualties," the Afghans fled the scene.[68] With the hammer gone, al-Qaeda defenders were free to turn their attention on the US anvil. Hundreds of US troops then became seriously engaged in one of the longest American firefights since Vietnam.[69] The Afghan allies did not return to the battle for several days, well after the most intense fighting was over. The battle was a coalition victory with al-Qaeda driven from the valley and an estimated 500 enemy killed. This success was incomplete since perhaps two-thirds of the enemy force slipped away on the numerous "rat trails" out of the mountains.

Conditions in Anaconda were extremely challenging. As at Tora Bora, terrain favored the enemy. The Afghan fighters faced the difficult task of advancing on enemy villages through interlocking fire with little terrain protection. There were sound reasons for using the AMFs in this way, but any judgment of Afghan performance at Anaconda must be tempered by the knowledge that the AMFs' leaders were not included in the operational planning for Anaconda even though their forces constituted a critical portion of the effort.

NA leaders were informed of the details of Anaconda only 72 hours before execution out of fear that the operation might be compromised by earlier disclosure.[70] American commanders faced a difficult choice since including the Afghans in the planning process potentially jeopardized operational security and American lives. The result was that the AMFs (and their US advisors) had little time to prepare for a difficult battle.

Additionally there was no formal plan for the possibility of the AMFs' failure. Maj Gen Franklin Hagenbeck, commanding the 10th Mountain Division and overall leader of the operation, claimed his staff was "intellectually prepared" for that contingency, but when asked if he had a branch plan, he replied "no."[71] This is especially significant in light of the crucial role planned for the Afghans and the limited forces available to reinforce the attack. At the time, there were still few US forces in Afghanistan. Hagenbeck's failure to develop a branch plan in anticipation of the AMFs' failure reflected a poor understanding of the intricacies of proxy warfare and ultimately jeopardized the entire operation.[72] Anaconda demonstrated that fog and friction will have greater effects on lesser-trained forces.

The Bottom Line on Indigenous Allies

Indigenous allies are simply tools of American foreign policy. Their salient attribute is that they are willing to fight with (and occasionally for) America. The tenuous nature of such alliances does not mean that the allies are either inherently reliable or unreliable. Instead, they possess unique qualities that planners must consider on a case-by-case basis. In Afghanistan the critical attribute of the Afghan rebels was simply their willingness to fight. As Colonel Rosengard observed, the primary qualification required of the Afghans at Anaconda was that "they could physically pick up a rifle and move toward the objective." At Tora Bora, "just the fact that [the AMFs] got us to that piece of ground was a success." Indigenous allies will not normally perform as well as American troops. Tactics, strategies, and operations should be designed to match the *allies' capabilities with the objectives of the United States*. Rosengard summed up the nature of proxy warfare with clarity: "If you gain credibility with an indigenous force and you bring a capability he doesn't have, he can achieve what he wants, and we can achieve what we want. It's a two way street, and it's often only good for today, not necessarily for tomorrow. The weakness is in the analysis of where those needs align . . . and that's on us."[73]

If Biddle is right and the relationship between the tactical skills of friendly forces *to those of the enemy* is the crucial consideration, then the relatively large presence of American troops in Anaconda should have produced much better results than those at Tora Bora. The enemy body count may have been higher at Anaconda, but the result was the same. The battle ended when the enemy decided to leave. To pin this failure on the Afghan allies is to obscure a lack of effective American planning. The skill of the allies is relevant, but it is their skill in relation *to the plan* that matters most.

When operations require complex fire and maneuver, an ally's tactical skill will indeed be critical. When an ally's role is simply to engage and fix the enemy, motivation may well be more important than skill. Requirements for success using the new model will vary depending on a host of factors. Trying to shoehorn an untrained force into normal US doctrine and battle plans is a mistake. Leaders must plan custom solutions to unique problems in application of the new model.[74]

The Precision Controversy

Since the first airman dropped the first bomb from an aircraft, controversy has existed as to the actual value of airpower's effects on the battlefield. The numerous successes of airpower in Desert Storm, Kosovo, and Afghanistan led many critics to caution that the PGMs are overrated since bombs by themselves are never sufficient for victory. Most Airmen will gladly put the sufficiency-of-airpower argument to rest. The PGMs are only weapons and will rarely be the sole means to victory. A more valid concern is posed by Max Boot: "The problem is that airpower's edge can be blunted by dispersing and concealing defensive forces; it takes ground forces to root out hidden troops."[75] In Enduring Freedom, the enemy often occupied unusually advantageous terrain to avoid destruction from the air.

Few would argue that the PGMs could find and destroy a notional "enemy company in the basement of a built up area" or "the twelve terrorists mixed with that crowd in the village market."[76] In Afghanistan, the PGMs were often only marginally effective against enemy fighters in deep tunnels, underground fortresses, or well-concealed caves. On the other hand, ground forces face similar problems against enemies using such fighting positions.

At the Qala-e-Gangi fortress near Mazar-e-Sharif, rioting prisoners held off air *and* ground forces alike for several days. "Entire ammunition payloads of multiple AC-130 gunships and no fewer than seven 2,000-pound JDAMs were expended. . . . Yet the defenders survived and continued to resist until succumbing only to the medieval technology of flooding by cold water."[77] While it is true that foot soldiers were ultimately required to ferret out the enemy, it is less known that allied fighters first tried igniting the underground tunnels with gasoline and firing "massive rockets down the drainage chutes" to force the enemy to capitulate. Even after flooding the tunnels of the fortress, 85 of the original 400 prisoners survived.[78] The action at Qala-e-Gangi demonstrates that no single type of force application, including land power, is sure to destroy the enemy.

Nonetheless, precision airpower provides key capabilities that enhance America's combat power. Precision airpower can often neutralize enemy forces, even if it does not destroy them. Enemy fighters forced to cower deep in mountain tunnels, underground fortresses, or caves are ineffective, isolated from their commanders, logistics, and fellow fighters. Friendly forces thus have the ability to effectively mass, fire, and maneuver, abilities successfully denied the enemy by precision airpower.

How prevalent are difficult conditions like those found in Afghanistan? Biddle asserted that "more than 26% of Somalia's land area is wooded or urban, as is more than 20% of the Sudan's, 34% of Georgia's or 46% of the Philippines."[79] To some, this may be daunting, but Airmen ought to be encouraged: 74, 80, 66, and 54 percent of those places, respectively, represent areas that may be appropriate for the use of precision munitions.

The concealment argument also assumes that conditions that protect the enemy from air weapons today will continue to do so in the future. This assumption ignores the progress of technology. Space-based radar, foliage-penetrating radar, micro-UAVs, miniaturized sensors, and earth-penetrating weapons will slowly whittle away at the enemy's ability to conceal.[80]

Part 3: Strategic Implications

Operations in northern Iraq and Afghanistan demonstrate that in the right circumstances, relatively few American ground troops can be deployed to achieve rather momentous effects. This has obvious meaning for future force structure, doctrine, and training, all addressed in the next chapter. Increased efficiency gained through the Afghan model has vast political implications that stem from its military efficiency. The model helps elected leaders preserve political capital and undertake more aggressive action while providing strategic flexibility, enhancing America's coercive power to deter unfriendly powers, and bettering chances for long-term political success in war.

Democracies are famously intolerant of prolonged wars and steady casualties. The new model relies on proxy forces, thereby entailing fewer American casualties. In Enduring Freedom, before the fall of the Taliban, total American casualties numbered fewer than 200, and only 22 of these soldiers died.[81] Most American citizens have no idea how many Afghans, Britons, Poles, or French lost their lives fighting the Taliban.

Utilizing a proxy force also enables US commanders to undertake more aggressive operations. Captain Swiecki observed after operations in northern Iraq that "conventional forces would not have accepted the unfavorable force ratios or the risks we took. We were able to take such risks because we were risking mainly Kurdish lives (sounds bad, but true) and we had faith in our ability to effectively use airpower, or slip away if things went dangerously wrong (we were only 8 Americans). American troops would not risk a movement to contact against an enemy with greater numbers and better equipment with only a trust in airpower and Iraqi cowardice to even the odds."[82] The fratricide incident at Debecka Pass also illustrates this double standard. Sixteen Kurdish freedom fighters died, and many more were wounded in the worst friendly-fire incident since Desert Storm. In spite of its gravity, most Americans (even in the military) are not aware of those losses.[83]

It is obvious that deploying 500 SOF troops is cheaper and faster than deploying a full US Army division. This is one reason why there were sufficient forces available to conduct simultaneous operations in Iraq and Afghanistan. Employment of the Afghan model probably telescoped the time requirement between the initiation of Enduring Freedom and Iraqi Freedom from perhaps a year or more down to months and also made possible the opening of a northern front in Iraqi Freedom.

The success of the Afghan model enhances America's deterrence in two complementary ways. First, it enhances the credibility of American coercion. After seeing US SOFs and airpower turn a loose collection of dissident factions into a powerful fighting force in Afghanistan, leaders of unfriendly nations might view American actions in a different light. Regimes may now have an incentive to provide conditions and means ("public goods"), so its people can improve the quality of their lives and avoid the repression and poverty that promotes rebellion.[84] Especially so if there is a threat of this kind of US intervention. Application of the model may also prove useful in preventing genocide in places like Rwanda or in protecting fledgling democracies around the globe. Most importantly, the model increases the chance that the United States can achieve objectives without necessarily committing to a full-scale military occupation of another nation, as experiences in Afghanistan demonstrate.

Finally, using the Afghan model increases the ability to achieve long-term political objectives. Clausewitz's notion that war and politics are inseparable is especially true in unconventional warfare. Utilizing indigenous forces to shoulder the majority of the ground fighting makes it much easier to appear as a liberator rather than a conqueror. A Kurdish fighter in Iraqi Freedom reflected this perspective when he said, "Before we only had the mountains as our friends . . . and now, thanks to God, we have the United States of America."[85] By fighting with the Afghans and the Kurds, the United States helped solidify postconflict support and minimized the chances of armed conflict with these factions. Had the United States attempted to fight in Afghanistan without the NA, or in Iraq without the Kurds, it would have increased the chances that these factions would now be actively opposing US presence in their countries rather than cooperating in rebuilding efforts.

Conclusion

In conclusion, a dramatic increase in American airpower capability is changing the dynamics of American foreign policy. In Operation Enduring Freedom, a handful of highly skilled SOF personnel brought to bear the world's premier air force against one of the world's worst armies, the Taliban. This unlikely alliance was able to topple their regime, reduce the terrorist threat to the world, and provide Afghanistan with a new chance to become a free and prosperous nation. Unfortunately, this force combination was born of necessity rather than a recognition of the increasing potential of precision airpower—the lack of good relations with Afghanistan's neighbors, geographic constraints, and a popular mandate to act quickly forced the US military to operate outside its normal doctrine and preferences.

In the wake of tremendous success in Afghanistan, skeptics argued that the success of SOFs and airpower in Afghanistan represented an anomaly. Events in Operation Iraqi Freedom proved them wrong—the model is valuable *and* repeatable. It was because of alliance politics that the military chose to use the new model in Iraq, and after two extremely successful campaigns, future planners must consider its use as a primary option rather than an emergency contingency procedure.

Notes

1. Bearden, "Afghanistan: Graveyard of Empires," 13–30.

2. Woodward, *Bush at War*, 43.

3. The Central Intelligence Agency was instrumental in this process. The agency had carefully cultivated contacts with Afghan rebels in the preceding years. In the months before 9/11, the agency had proposed increasing aid to the Northern Alliance in hopes of deposing the Taliban. Woodward offers perhaps the best account of the early stages of Operation Enduring Freedom in Woodard, *Bush at War*. For a wider political view of America's thinking on methods of dealing with terrorists in Afghanistan, see Benjamin and Simon, *Age of Sacred Terror*, 326–49.

4. The terms *model*, *new model*, and *Afghan model* will be used interchangeably.

5. Dries, "Future Counterland Operations," 19.

6. Priest, "In War, Mud Huts."

7. An SF Operational Detachment Alpha, or "A" team, normally consists of 12 personnel. Bruner, Bolkcom, and O'Rourke, *Special Operations Forces*, 1.

8. Newman, *JFK and Vietnam*, 160.

9. See Rosenau, *Special Operations Forces*, n.p.

10. Evidence of this pressure was visible in a National Security Council meeting 10 days after the 9/11 attacks when President Bush noted, "We've got to start showing results." Woodward, *Bush at War*, 113.

11. Ibid., 115.

12. Col Kevin Weddle, USA War College; Col Mark Bontraeger, USAF Task Force Enduring Look; and Dr. Richard Stewart, USA Center of Military History, interview by the author, Washington, DC, 24 October 2004. There is no documented evidence of these force caps, but military leaders insist that verbal guidance was issued. Many believe that Secretary of Defense Donald Rumsfeld deliberately did not publish such restrictions to avoid the possibility of being accused of providing the military with insufficient resources if events soured (as happened in 1994 in Somalia). Lt Gen Franklin "Buster" Hagenbeck stated, "I'm not sure if this [the force cap] was poor staff work" or secretary of defense policy but asserted that force caps were in effect. Lt Gen Franklin Hagenbeck, interview by Maj Mark Davis, USA, Washington, DC, 28 January 2003.

13. Woodward, *Bush at War*, 115–16.

14. Col Mark Rosengard, director of operations, Task Force Dagger, interview by the author, 27 February 2004.

15. Vego, "What Can We Learn?"

16. Jalali, "Afghanistan," 86.

17. Lt Gen Mike Short, interview by the author, 12 November 2003. Bob Woodward's account lends credence to this claim. According to Woodward, the Pentagon was sluggish in presenting meaningful options to policy makers. See Woodward, *Bush at War*.

18. Grant, *Afghan Air War*, 15.

19. Beaumont et al., "Rout of the Taliban."

20. Bonin, "First Year," 30.

21. Ibid.

22. Ricks and Struck, "US Troops Coordinating Airstrikes."

23. Biddle, "Afghanistan and the Future of Warfare," 8–12.

24. Decker to the author, letter.

25. Chipman, "Air Power," 34–45. The campaign for Mazar-e-Sharif consisted of several engagements, so calculating the exact force ratio is difficult. These numbers reflect the forces involved during the final advance on the city. While the numbers are likely low on both sides, the percentages are probably accurate.

26. Ibid., 38.

27. Andrade, "Battle for Mazar-e-Sharif," 4.

28. Briefing, Entwistle, chart 22.

29. Exact numbers are elusive, but it is safe to say that there were a little over 1,000 US conventional forces in Afghanistan when the Taliban fell. Bonin, "First Year," 33; and Stewart, US Army in Afghanistan.

30. Secretary of State Colin Powell, quoted in Schmitt and Dao, "Use of Air Power."

31. Vego, "What Can We Learn?"

32. Murray and Scales, Iraq War, 186–90. The "Green Line" was a de facto border within Iraq that roughly separated Kurdish and Iraqi territory.

33. Exact numbers are elusive. See Aydintasbas, "Kurdish Dilemma"; and "Kurdish Resistance Forces."

34. Operational Detachment A Teams 391 and 392, for example, were expecting 200 Kurds for an operation, and approximately 80 showed up. See Naylor, "Nightmare at Debecka."

35. Swiecki to the author, e-mail.

36. Ibid.

37. Naylor, "Nightmare at Debecka."

38. Carver, memorandum for record.

39. Ibid. A battalion-sized element is approximately 1,000 troops.

40. Ba'ath Party enforcers often inspired continued resistance. At the battle of Debecka Pass, Iraqis attempting to surrender were summarily executed. SFC Frank Antenori, telephone interview by the author, 18 February 2004. See also Murray and Scales, Iraq War, 189.

41. Swiecki to the author, e-mail.

42. Antenori, interview.

43. Ibid. The Iraqis parked their armor next to an elevated roadway, leaving only the top of the tanks visible to the SF teams. Unfortunately, ground-directed-laser energy passed over the turrets due to the "graze" angle generated by a combination of Iraqi placement and friendly-troop position. As a result, the laser "spot" impacted the ground well beyond the target. The LGBs functioned properly, but since the laser was not reflecting on the targets, the tanks survived.

44. Naylor, "Nightmare at Debecka."

45. Antenori, interview.

46. Swiecki to the author, e-mail.

47. Biddle, "Afghanistan and the Future of Warfare," 43.

48. US Marines had established a small forward base near Kandahar, and only a reinforced company of the 10th Mountain Division was available at Bagram and Mazar-e-Sharif. See Stewart, *US Army in Afghanistan*, 26.

49. Bonin, "First Year," 34; and Stewart, *US Army in Afghanistan*, 24.

50. Haas to the author, letter.

51. Stewart, *US Army in Afghanistan*, 24.

52. Glasser, "Battle of Tora Bora."

53. Ibid.

54. Ibid. "Hazrat Ali is very opportunistic, taking money from our side, and also the Al-Qaeda folks," according to an unnamed Western diplomat.

55. Donnelly, "Fighting Terror."

56. Stewart, *US Army in Afghanistan*, 26.

57. Arostegui, "Search for bin Laden."

58. Bruce Pirnie (RAND, Washington, DC), interview by the author, 22 October 2003.

59. Donnelly, "Fighting Terror." In addition, Lt Col Christopher Haas and Col Mark Rosengard confirmed this. Haas to the author, letter; and Rosengard, interview.

60. Haas to the author, letter.

61. Donnelly, "Fighting Terror."

62. Lambeth, *Air Power against Terror*, 146.

63. Colonel Haas related that the enormity of the task presented a logistical and tactical problem that the Marines were unwilling to tackle at this stage of the war. Haas to the author, letter.

64. Biddle, "Afghanistan and the Future of Warfare," chart 13.

65. Rosengard, interview. Haas added, "Even our best [infantry divisions] would have had serious, serious difficulties in this area." Haas to the author, letter.

66. Donnelly, "Fighting Terror." Haas noted that Ali's main motivations were money, a preference for television coverage, and the prestige associated with US support. Haas to the author, letter.

67. Both Rosengard and Haas asserted that US Army planners were unsurprised by the AMFs failure at Tora Bora. Rosengard, interview; and Haas to the author, letter.

68. College of Aerospace Doctrine, Research and Education (CADRE), "Operation Anaconda Case Study," 26. Although not known at the time, the AMF suffered "friendly fire" from an AC-130 on the scene.

69. Dr. Richard Kugler, interview by the author, Washington, DC, October 2003. Kugler likened this situation to Custer's defeat at the Little Big Horn. Kugler, Baranick, and Binnendijk, "*Anaconda's Lessons*," 26.

70. CADRE, "Operation Anaconda Case Study," 26. Confirmed by Colonel Rosengard. Rosengard, interview.

71. Hagenbeck, interview.

72. Anaconda was a rare example of conventional forces integrating SOFs into conventional tactics. Ibid. This may explain why the plan for Afghan allies seemed to suffer from differing expectations. Colonel Rosengard, an SF leader responsible for training the Afghans, asserted that TF Dagger had considered

the AMFs' failure as a branch plan and had war-gamed that contingency. "We knew that they would go until they were turned away and we knew at some point that was likely to happen." Rosengard, interview. It is not clear, however, that General Hagenbeck shared this expectation.

73. Rosengard, interview.

74. The Battle of Cowpens during the American Revolution offers a poignant example of utilizing poorly trained troops to a positive effect. American brigadier general Daniel Morgan, noting that militia "always broke and ran," devised a plan in which the militia would "break and run under orders." For more detail, see Treacy, *Prelude to Yorktown*; or Roberts, *Battle of Cowpens*.

75. Boot, "New American Way of War," 55.

76. Van Riper, quoted in Lambeth, *Transformation of American Air Power*, 301.

77. Biddle, "Afghanistan and the Future of Warfare," 35.

78. Harding, "Battle for Afghanistan," n.p.

79. Biddle, "Afghanistan and the Future of Warfare," 32.

80. See Vick et al., *Enhancing Air Power's Contribution*.

81. Bonin, "First Year," 38.

82. Swiecki to the author, e-mail.

83. Naylor, "Nightmare at Debecka."

84. See Lichbach, *Rebel's Dilemma*, for an in-depth discussion of public goods.

85. Dehghanpisheh, "Now We Have America," 35.

Chapter 5

Implications

The armies themselves, their operations, their strategy, and even their tactics are little different from what they were in the days of the Romans.

—Billy Mitchell

The titanic clash of mighty armies is becoming an obsolete paradigm in the western world's compendium of acceptable military options. Ground forces themselves will not become obsolete; but they will have to evolve. They must become lighter and more mobile. While retaining true warfighting capability, they should concentrate more on operations at the lower end of the range of military operations where interests every bit as vital to the nation as those protected by classic attrition warfare reside. And as distasteful as it might be to a land force centric command structure used to being at the center of major joint force operations, they will often be required to play an unaccustomed, but vital supporting role to national aerospace power.

—Gene Myers
Joint Aerospace Power:
A New National Strategy

In the preceding chapters, this paper has shown that airpower is changing the face of modern war. Improvements in stealth, precision, and persistence have dramatically altered the relative utility of air and ground power. While it is popular to characterize recent progress as a revolution in military affairs or a new way of war, such are secondary to the fundamental issue at hand.

Airpower capabilities have grown since 1991:

1. America's enemies cannot mass without fear of certain destruction.

2. Fewer troops are required in modern combat.

3. Policy makers enjoy increased options due to airpower's flexibility and lethality.

These trends are of enormous importance to America, and airpower's ascendance in the air/ground-power relationship has three important implications for America:

1. Since precision airpower enables US commanders to accomplish more with less during combat, the DOD must reassess military force structure.

2. The ongoing transformation movement within the services must be coordinated (not just deconflicted) to reflect the new relationship between air and ground power.

3. The services must adapt their doctrine and training mechanisms to take full advantage of recent growth in airpower capabilities.

Of these three imperatives, force structure will be most controversial, so this subject will be discussed first.

Army Force Structure

The American military must make significant reductions in its heavy ground forces. Since the demise of the Soviet Union, America has had little practical use for its heavy divisions. In both wars with Iraq, the United States has deployed far more armor than necessary to secure victory. This superfluous force structure has had a deleterious effect on American capability, absorbing resources better used to train and equip America's Army to face more threatening scenarios. Unfortunately, US ground forces, "while somewhat slimmed down, [are] still trained, equipped, and structured to fight a peer enemy (Russia) in a bipolar world."[1]

An enemy force that cannot mass will increasingly disperse, conceal, and resort to tactics of the weak—instances where it makes little sense to have a force designed primarily to fight large-scale, frontal operations. Elements of US ground power, such as main battle tanks, though still relevant, are clearly less important than they were at the height of the Cold War.[2] America's tank inventory is well over 4,000 strong—an extremely high number given the state of the threat and the capabilities of joint airpower.[3]

Some experts caution that replacing heavy forces is a time-consuming process that could leave the United States vulnerable in the future, or they argue that maintaining a massive armored force is critical in case of major war with a similarly armed opponent. William Hawkins warned, "The lesson that should be learned by those who have been urging a restructuring of the US military toward lighter forces, whether for peacekeeping duties during the years of the Clinton Administration or anti-terrorism operations now, is that it is difficult to rapidly upgrade forces designed for the low end of the conflict spectrum to handle larger wars. And it is usually the larger wars that have the higher stakes."[4]

Hawkins's observation that larger wars are more important is certainly correct, but his warning that heavy forces are difficult to reconstitute is essentially fearmongering. Heavy equipment withdrawn from the Army's inventory, preserved in "mothball" status, could be returned to service in a relatively short period. The notion that a peer competitor will suddenly appear with conventional power on par with America's is unrealistic.[5] It will take any potential adversary years to develop armored forces comparable to our own, and such efforts are unlikely to escape detection. Maintaining excess tanks in ready storage will also discourage hostile efforts to achieve heavy ground-force parity. This allows the United States to tailor its forces to deal with realistic threats. Moreover, so long as the United States maintains airpower supremacy, there is little incentive for any nation to seek to build a larger, better, Cold War–style armored force. Enemies cannot mass in the face of American airpower.

With the demise of the Soviet Union, it has become popular to think of China as America's next major adversary. Large population, communist ideology, and vast economic potential make China a convenient bogeyman. But using the threat of China to justify a large armored force represents faulty reasoning. While it is true that China seeks a greater role in Asia, it is less clear that China wishes to replace the Soviet Union as an exporter of communism. Instead, "preparing for a potential conflict in the Taiwan Strait is the primary driver for China's military modernization."[6] Recent Chinese modernization efforts have emphasized accelerating acquisition of antiaccess technologies such as diesel submarines, destroyers, smaller-surface combatants, surface-to-air missile systems, and jet fighters.[7] These initiatives indicate a Chinese recognition that American land- and carrier-based airpower poses a far greater threat to China than massive American armored forces.

Maintaining a heavy US force due to fears of Chinese expansionism ignores geopolitical realities in Asia. Pakistan, India, and the CIS seem unlikely targets for Chinese aggression, largely because each owns a nuclear deterrence. In the unlikely event China chose to invade Myanmar, Laos, or Vietnam, armor would be of little use. Harsh mountain ranges and thick jungles would funnel this hypothetical, massive armored force to relatively few instances of open terrain, making it an easy target for precision airpower. Simply put, a large armored force in China will never be a threat to US interests.

There is little justification for maintaining inordinately large, heavy ground forces. As long as America maintains air superiority, the era of the tank is over. Tanks may still be necessary, but not in the numbers America now possesses. The US military must draw down some of its heavy forces and invest in force structure that matches likely threats of the early twenty-first century.

This is not to suggest that the size of the Army needs to be greatly reduced. Current experience in Iraq indicates that so long as invasion and occupation are foreign policy options, the US Army is likely as small as it should be. In fact, the Army may be too small to support America's interests in nation building. This does not mitigate the need to transform the Army, however. The Army must embrace missions at the lower spectrum of conflict: counterinsurgency, peace enforcement, peacekeeping, and nation building.

Amazingly, at the height of Operation Iraqi Freedom, the Army announced that it would close the Peacekeeping Institute of the Army War College, ostensibly to "save money and get more active duty officers serving with troops in the field."[8] A political firestorm ensued over the decision, and ultimately, the institute received increased staffing and funding. US experiences in Haiti, Somalia, Bosnia, Kosovo, Afghanistan, and Iraq prove that counterinsurgency and peacekeeping missions are here to stay.

Preparing for war is not the same as preparing for peace. In Iraq the United States has suffered far more casualties at the hands of insurgents than in the brief campaign against Saddam's army.[9] Unfortunately, the Army is not organized, trained, or equipped for peacekeeping and nation-building missions with the same competency it conducts war. As one observer in Iraq noted, "For most of these war-toughened young Americans, the Arab and Islamic culture they must penetrate to ferret out the insurgents remains a mystery all these months later. They're professional soldiers, smooth and sure at urban fighting tactics. But once inside the houses, pressed into a counterinsurgency role they've never been trained for, they improvise, often amateurishly. Until a month ago, they didn't even have an Arab translator."[10]

Retired Marine general Anthony Zinni observed, "Right now the question that has to be answered is, does our military expand its role beyond the military aspect, or will we continue to stick it with this mission without the resources, the training, the cooperation from others, or the lack of authority needed to get the job done?"[11] Establishing permanent peace-enforcement divisions will allow the DOD to develop a core of expertise in this area and provide the United States a much-improved capability in postcombat situations. Special forces, which have long been the repository of nation-building expertise, are too scarce to execute such operations on a grand scale.

Unfortunately, the public may be learning the wrong lessons from events in Iraq. Due to a lack of embedded media reporting and the impotence of the Iraqi air force, the war seemed to be almost exclusively a land campaign. In testimony before Congress, retired major general Robert Scales asserted, "Neither the air force nor the navy confronts an enemy with technologically sophisticated forces at sea or in the air. Consequently, the function of those services is now mostly to project and deliver ground forces to a particular theater and then support those forces with precision killing power."[12]

Over a 12-year period, airpower (land and sea based) crushed, contained, and ultimately destroyed the Iraqi army. Airpower enabled the swift march to Baghdad; Airmen destroyed targets in front of the advance, protected its flanks, and provided real-time ISR that was critical to the success of the ground war. In Iraq, due in large part to airpower, the primary challenge had less to do with direct combat between ground forces than with restoring order, maintaining security, and "winning hearts and minds." These skills desperately need sharpening in today's military.

Congress recently voted to increase Army personnel strength to fulfill extended deployments in Iraq and Afghanistan. America must be careful in allocating money and resources. The time is right to update Army force structure to ensure that in the future America could win the peace as easily as winning the war. But peacekeeping forces are "cobbled together," and as DOD transformation chief Arthur Cebrowski recently noted, "This issue is too important and too hard to rely on cobbling."[13]

Service Transformation

Service transformation must reflect the increased capability of airpower, but early indications are that the Army continues to ignore the lessons of the past decade. Officially the Army is taking steps to transform into a lighter, more deployable force, but full transformation to the "objective force" is to take some 30 years. This three-decade approach is problematic because the security environment in 2030 is simply unknown, and by then a peer competitor could emerge on a scale sufficient to threaten America. It will likely take that long, and force-structure requirements will certainly change. In contrast, the security environment of today is much clearer. Lighter, more-versatile forces are needed immediately, and the Army must accelerate its transformation.

Airmen are not immune from transformational foot-dragging. The Army of the future will be lighter and more mobile; it will possess less-organic firepower and, consequently, be more reliant on air support. It is not clear, however, that Air Force transformation accounts for this new reliance. The *Air Force Transformation Roadmap* claims that in fiscal years 04–09, the Air Force will spend only 23 percent of its Total Obligation Authority on joint combat forces such as CAS fighters and gunships; loitering, indirect fires; and advanced air-to-ground munitions. Forty-one percent will go to critical joint-force enablers such as air and space command, control, communications, computers, intelligence, surveillance, and reconnaissance; airlift; and tankers.[14]

This glowing statement seems encouraging, but lingering questions remain. Joint audiences recognize the CAS fighters referred to above as the F-35 Joint Strike Fighters (JSF). Whether the F-35 is just window dressing on the Air Force's part or a sincere belief that the JSF is an aircraft optimized for CAS remains to be seen. Traditionally the Army has had little use for fast CAS platforms (JSF will be a Mach 1.8 "fast" CAS aircraft), preferring relatively slow, survivable, well-armed airplanes like the (Mach 0.3) A-10. The success of transformation depends on trust: if more credit is given to airpower, the Air Force must ensure that follow-on systems are truly "born joint" and not "need for speed" dream jets shoehorned into a joint requirement.

Service-transformation efforts offer some hope, but much work remains. A recent Army briefing spoke of "taking advantage of joint air superiority and precision munitions capabilities," and the Air Force speaks of a commitment to "joint enablers." It remains to be seen, whether this is simply rhetoric: the term *airpower* does not appear at all in the Army document, and "objective force" is listed only once in the Air Force road map.[15]

Doctrine and Training

As the relationship between air and ground power continues to evolve, so must the roles of each component. In light of airpower's increasing capabilities, what is the role of the land component? Since the end of the Vietnam War, traditional combat using heavy ground forces has been rare, consuming just 100 hours in Desert Storm and some three weeks during Iraqi Freedom. Ground forces hold the enemy and force him to mass (as in Desert Storm or Iraqi Freedom) or locate and dislodge him from concealed positions (as in Enduring Freedom). As Doug Mason observed, "Put simply, the ground force . . . needs to present a credible one-dimensional ground threat to the opposing force. A 'credible' threat does not mean that the United States must attain a numerical advantage on the ground, or even numerical parity."[16] Now, commanders must actively plan to use ground forces to shape the air war rather than vice versa.[17] This philosophy is not air-centric hubris; instead, it is born of a "principle that [airpower] can save lives and provide theater commanders with a more effective and responsible way of employing force than through head to head, manpower intensive combat on the ground."[18]

This is not to suggest that ground power is unimportant; in fact, the opposite is true. The wars in Kosovo, Afghanistan, and Iraq demonstrated that the land component is an integral part of the air campaign. As airpower forces the enemy to disperse and conceal, boots on the ground will be more important than ever. However, the traditional paradigm in which heavy armored forces engage in massive tank battles is outdated—a reality that joint doctrine should reflect.

The 1990s saw air-intensive conflict in Europe, yet until 2000 the theater commander was an Army general. In fact, since the creation of the Air Force, only two Airmen have served as the joint force commanders (JFC).[19] This disparity results in suboptimal employment of airpower. To enhance the application of airpower, the DOD must select Airmen more often as geographic combatant commanders.

At the operational level of war, the JFCs should also designate the joint force air component commander (JFACC) more often as the "supported" commander during war.[20] Jack Egginton suggested that "ideally, the JFACC supervises the orchestration of a jointly devised and agreed upon general scheme of maneuver aimed at promoting [air] as the primary killing mechanism without subjecting the ground force to undue risk."[21] In Iraqi Freedom, Gen Tommy R. Franks (the JFC) designated the JFACC as the supported commander for operations in western Iraq. Yet few Iraqi forces opposed the United States. Control was largely ceded to the JFACC to maximize aerial operations against Iraqi Scud missile launchers. In the future, the JFCs must consider appointing the JFACC as the supported commander in operations such as Enduring Freedom and those on the northern front in Iraq where airpower is the dominant maneuver force.

With great power comes great responsibility. The Air Force must make a commitment to preparing its officers for joint warfare. Airmen are notoriously unfamiliar with joint doctrine—a fact that can only hamper the effective advocacy and employment of airpower. Similarly, the Air Force must take steps to educate its members in the art of maneuver warfare. Currently, the average Air Force officer is not exposed to joint or sister-service doctrine until he or she is a field-grade officer. The result of this trend is that the Air Force does not maintain a comprehensive vision of warfare that includes naval and ground power, whereas the other services have systematic, if limited, doctrinal approaches to airpower. The new relationship between air and ground power requires a certain measure of trust from the sea and ground components.

Conclusion

Over the past quarter century, American airpower has developed at an amazing pace. Unfortunately, interservice rhetoric, parochialism, and bureaucratic wrangling have obscured a salient fact: Airpower has evolved so much that it now dominates the air/ground-power relationship. Increasing accuracy, lethality, and political utility have made airpower America's most useful military force. In sum, this is the age of airpower.

The new relationship between airpower and ground power has important meaning for America. The DOD can reduce the number of direct combat troops in its ground forces. Heavy divisions, while still relevant, are less important than in the past. The Army must realize the efficiencies gained through airpower to embrace its most likely missions—peacekeeping and nation building. These missions are vital capabilities in the post–Cold War environment—and in areas where the US military is simply not good enough.

It is increasingly clear that in the future, enemy tactics will respond to American capabilities. One CIS military commentator noted, "The Americans have rewritten the textbook and every country had better take note."[22] Indeed, the most successful efforts against US forces in the last decade have been instances where the enemy dispersed. The Serb army survived largely intact in Kosovo, and al-Qaeda suffered large casualties only when it massed in the Shah-e-Khot Valley. Iraqi resisters have been far more successful in civilian clothes than in uniform. Antiaccess, asymmetric warfare, and terrorist strategies are much more viable than large, conventional confrontations. In short, enemy training, organization, and equipment will reflect the lessons of airpower, even if America's force structure does not.

The DOD must not allow itself to stagnate in this era of unrivaled superiority. Ignoring the changing face of warfare is a costly proposition. Sun Tzu warned, "One who knows neither the enemy nor himself will invariably be defeated in every engagement."[23] The American military must not turn a blind eye to the changing relationship between air and ground power lest future soldiers pay for this shortsightedness in blood.

Notes

1. Bickel, "Buying Smart."

2. For an excellent discussion, see Macgregor, *Transformation under Fire*.

3. Nichols to the author, letter. Blechman and Lum place this number at 6,700 tanks, but that is likely exaggerated. See "Rethinking Transformation," 38–42.

4. Hawkins, "What Not to Learn," 24–32.

5. Restoring mothballed equipment is a relatively straightforward process. Training the personnel required to operate these tanks requires longer lead time. Maintaining an armor force (albeit smaller) will ensure that US tank doctrine remains cutting edge.

6. US DOD, "2003 Annual Report."

7. Ibid.

8. Kelly, "Iraq Provides."

9. There were 139 troops killed during "major combat operations," but since 1 May 2003, the US military death toll in Iraq has risen to over 2,247. See US DOD, "Operation Iraqi Freedom Military Deaths through April 30, 2003;" and US DOD, "Operation Iraqi Freedom Military Deaths since May 1, 2003."

10. Hirsh, "Blood and Honor," 38.

11. Zinni, "How Do We Overhaul?"

12. US House of Representatives, *Statement by MG (RET) Robert H. Scales, Jr.*

13. Quoted in Graham, "Pentagon Considers."

14. Headquarters US Air Force, *USAF Transformation Flight Plan*, 15.

15. The Army uses the term *joint fires* in describing airpower. See "2004 Army Transformation Roadmap." In the 176-page USAF document, there are zero instances of the terms *Interim Brigade Combat Team*, *Brigade Combat Team*, or *Stryker Brigade*. See *The U.S. Air Force Transformation Flight Plan*.

16. Mason, "New American Way of War?" 13.

17. For more information, see Jinnette, "Employing an Air Maneuver Force," 15–17.

18. Khalilzad and Ochmanek, "Rethinking US Defense Policy,"43–64; and quoted in Lambeth, *Transformation of American Air Power*, 289.

19. Gen Joseph Ralston served as commander of US European Command and supreme allied commander, Europe, from 2000 to 2003. Gen Lauris Norstad served in the same capacity from 1956 to 1962. In fairness, subordinate commanders have been Airmen. See US European Command Web Site, "European Command Leadership." For example, Airmen commanded Joint Task Force Southwest Asia (JTF-SWA) (responsible for Operation Southern Watch) from its inception. For a history of JTF-SWA, see Web Site of GlobalSecurity.org, "Operation Southern Watch."

20. Joint Publication 1-02, *Department of Defense Dictionary*, "**supported commander** (DOD)"

The commander having primary responsibility for all aspects of a task assigned by the Joint Strategic Capabilities Plan or other joint operation planning authority. In the context of joint operation planning, this term refers to the commander who prepares operation plans or operation orders in response to requirements of the Chairman of the Joint Chiefs of Staff. 2. In the context of a support command relationship, the commander who receives assistance from another commander's force or capabilities, and who is responsible for ensuring that the supporting commander understands the assistance required (517).

21. Quoted in Jinnette, "Employing an Air Maneuver Force," 16.
22. Pashentsev, cited in Weir, "Iraqi Defeat Jolts Russian Military."
23. Sun Tzu, *Art of War*, 179.

Bibliography

After-Action Report. "3rd Infantry Division (Mechanized): Operation Iraqi Freedom," October 2003.

Ambrose, Steven. *D-Day: The Climactic Battle of World War II.* New York: Simon and Schuster, 1994.

Andradé, Dale. "The Battle for Mazar-e-Sharif, October–November 2001." Information paper. Washington, DC: US Army Center of Military History, 1 March 2002.

Arostegui, Martin. "The Search for bin Laden." *Insight Magazine,* 12 August 2002. http://www.insightmag.com/news/2002/09/02/World/Special.Reportthe.Search.For.Osama.Bin.Laden-260506.shtml (accessed 10 May 2004).

Arquilla, John, and David Ronfeldt. *Swarming and the Future of Conflict.* Santa Monica, CA: RAND, 2000.

Aspin, Les, and William Dickinson. *Defense for a New Era: Lessons of the Persian Gulf War.* Washington, DC: Brassey's, 1992.

Aydintasbas, Aysla. "The Kurdish Dilemma." *Salon Magazine,* 6 September 2002. http://www.salon.com/people/interview/2002/09/06/salih/ (accessed 7 May 2004).

Bearden, Milton. "Afghanistan: Graveyard of Empires." *Foreign Affairs,* November–December 2001, 13–30.

Beaumont, Peter, Kamal Ahmed, Ed Vulliamy, Jason Burke, Chris Stephen, Tim Judah, and Paul Harris. "The Rout of the Taliban." *Observer,* 18 November 2001. http://observer.guardian.co.uk/afghanistan/story/0,1501,596923,00.html (accessed 20 October 2004).

Benjamin, Daniel, and Steven Simon. *The Age of Sacred Terror: Radical Islam's War against America.* New York: Random House, 2002.

Bickel, Keith B. "Buying Smart." *Blueprint Magazine,* January 2000. http://www.ppionline.org/ppi_ci.cfm?knlgAreaID=124&subsecID=159&contentID=1129 (accessed 6 February 2006).

Biddle, Stephen. "Afghanistan and the Future of Warfare: Implications for Army and Defense Policy." Carlisle Barracks, PA: Strategic Studies Institute, US Army War College, 2002. http://www.carlisle.army.mil/usassi/welcome.htm (accessed 27 October 2004).

Bin, Alberto, Richard Hill, and Archer Jones. *Desert Storm: A Forgotten War.* Westport, CT: Praeger, 1998.

Blechman, Barry M., and Zachary Lum. "Rethinking Transformation: Army's Ground-Power-Dominant Concept Undercuts Potential Full-Dimensional US Warfighting Capabilities." *Armed Forces Journal International* 138, no. 8 (March 2001): 38–42.

Bonin, John A. "The First Year: US Army Forces Central Command during Operation Enduring Freedom." Case study. Carlisle Barracks, PA: US Army War College, 2002.

Boot, Max. "The New American Way of War." *Foreign Affairs*, July–August 2003, 41–58.

Bowie, Christopher, Fred Frostic, Kevin N. Lewis, John Lund, David A. Ochmanek, and Philip Propper. *The New Calculus: Analyzing Airpower's Changing Role in Joint Theater Campaigns.* Santa Monica, CA: RAND, 1993.

Briefing. Alan Vick, Adam Grissom, Karl Mueller, David Orletsky, Bruce Pirnie. Subject: "Beyond CAS: Forging a New Air-Ground Partnership," circulated by e-mail, October 2003.

———. Col Tom Entwistle, Task Force Enduring Look. Subject: Operation Enduring Freedom Preliminary Lessons, October 2002.

———. Headquarters Department of the Army. Deputy Chief of Staff (DCS), G-3 (Operations and Plans). Media Roundtable. Subject: Building Army Capabilities, 17 February 2004, slide 14.

———. Maj Gen David Deptula, School of Advanced Air and Space Studies. Subject: "Some Observations on Modern Warfare: Then and Now—Desert Storm, OEF, OIF." Maxwell AFB, AL, 15 December 2003.

Bruner, Edward F., Christopher Bolkcom, and Ronald O'Rourke. *Special Operations Forces in Operation Enduring Freedom: Background and Issues for Congress.* Washington, DC: Congressional Research Service, 15 October 2001.

Carver, Capt Eric, USA, commander. Operational Detachment Alpha (ODA) 065, C Company, 2nd Battalion, 10th Special Forces Group. Memorandum for record, 16 April 2003.

Chipman, Cdr Don, USN, retired. "Air Power and the Battle for Mazar-e-Sharif." *Air Power History* 50, no. 1 (Spring 2003): 34–45.

Clausewitz, Carl von. *On War.* Edited and translated by Michael Howard and Peter Paret. Princeton, NJ: Princeton University Press, 1976.

Cohen, Eliot et al. *Gulf War Air Power Survey.* Vol. 2, *Operations and Effects and Effectiveness.* Washington, DC: Government Printing Office, 1993.

College of Aerospace Doctrine, Research and Education (CADRE). "Operation Anaconda Case Study." Internal case study. Maxwell AFB, AL: CADRE, 2003.

Conetta, Carl. "Catastrophic Interdiction: Air Power and the Collapse of the Iraqi Field Army in the 2003 War." Briefing Memo no. 30. Cambridge, MA: Commonwealth Institute, Project on Defense Alternatives, 26 September 2003. http://www.comw.org/pda/ (accessed 10 February 2004).

Cordesman, Anthony H. *The Iraq War: Strategy, Tactics, and Military Lessons.* Washington, DC: Center for Strategic and International Studies, 2003.

————. *The Lessons and Non-Lessons of the Air and Missile Campaign in Kosovo.* Westport, CT: Praeger, 2001.

————. *The Lessons of Afghanistan: War Fighting, Intelligence, Force Transformation, Counterproliferation and Arms Control.* Washington, DC: Center for Strategic and International Studies, 12 May 2003.

Cordesman, Anthony H., and Abraham R. Wagner. *The Lessons of Modern War.* Vol. 1, *The Arab-Israeli Conflicts, 1973–1989.* Boulder, CO: Westview Press, 1990.

————. *The Lessons of Modern War.* Vol. 2, *The Iran-Iraq War.* Boulder, CO: Westview Press, 1990.

————. *The Lessons of Modern War.* Vol. 4, *The Gulf War.* Boulder, CO: Westview Press, 1996.

Correll, John T. *Strategy, Requirements and Forces: The Rising Imperative of Air and Space Power.* Arlington, VA: Aerospace Education Foundation, 2003.

Decker, MSgt Bart. To the author. Letter, personal correspondence, 15 January 2004.

Dehghanpisheh, Babak. "Now We Have America." *Newsweek,* 7 April 2003, 35. http://search.epnet.com/direct.asp?an=9406938&db=aph (accessed 27 October 2003).

Deptula, Brig Gen David. *Effects-Based Operations: Change in the Nature of Warfare.* Arlington, VA: Aerospace Education

Foundation, 2001. http://www.aef.org/pub/psbook.pdf (accessed 19 April 2004).

Deptula, Maj Gen David, Col Gary Crowder, and Maj George L. Stamper Jr. "Direct Attack: Enhancing Counterland Doctrine and Joint Air-Ground Operations." *Air and Space Power Journal* 17, no. 4 (Winter 2003): 5–12.

Donnelly, John. "Fighting Terror—The Military Campaign; How US Strategy in Tora Bora Failed: Deals by Afghan Allies May Have Let Al Qaeda Leaders Escape." *Boston Globe*, 10 February 2002.

Douhet, Giulio. *The Command of the Air.* Translated by Dino Ferrari, 1942. Reprint, North Stratford, NH: Ayer Company, 1999.

Dries, William D. "Future Counterland Operations: Common Lessons from Three Conflicts." Master's thesis, US Army School of Advanced Military Studies, Fort Leavenworth, KS, 2003.

Ewing, Michael. *Khe Sanh.* New York: Bantam Books, 1987.

Givens, Lt Col Robert P. *Turning the Vertical Flank: Airpower as a Maneuver Force in the Theater Campaign.* CADRE Paper no. 13. Maxwell AFB, AL: Air University Press, June 2002.

Glasser, Susan B. "The Battle of Tora Bora: Secrets, Money, Mistrust." *Washington Post,* 10 February 2002.

GlobalSecurity.org Web Site. "Operation Southern Watch." http://www.globalsecurity.org/military/ops/southern_watch.htm (accessed 8 March 2006).

Gordon, Michael. "US Air Raids in '02 Prepared for War in Iraq." *New York Times,* 20 July 2003.

Gordon, Michael R., and Gen Bernard E. Trainor. *The Generals' War: The Inside Story of the Conflict in the Gulf.* Boston: Little, Brown and Company, 1995.

Graham, Bradley. "Pentagon Considers Creating Postwar Peacekeeping Forces." *Washington Post,* 24 November 2003.

Graham, Bradley, and Vernon Loeb. "An Air War of Might, Coordination, and Risks." *Washington Post,* 27 April 2003, final ed.

Grant, Rebecca. *The Afghan Air War.* Arlington, VA: Aerospace Education Foundation, 2002.

———. *Gulf War II: Air and Space Power Led the Way.* Arlington, VA: Aerospace Education Foundation, 2003.

———. "The War Nobody Expected." *Air Force Magazine* 85, no. 4 (April 2002): 34–40. http://www.afa.org/magazine/april2002/0402airwar.asp (accessed 20 October 2003).

Grier, Peter. "The Combination that Worked." *Air Force Magazine* 85, no. 4 (April 2002): 30–32. http://www.afa.org/magazine/april2002/0402combo.asp (accessed 27 October 2003).

Grosso, Maj, USA, commander, Operational Detachment Bravo (ODB) 060, C Company, 2nd Battalion, 10th Special Forces Group. Memorandum for record, 3 May 2003.

Haag, SSgt Jason L. "OIF Veterans Discuss Lessons." *Air Force Link*, 31 July 2003. http://www.af.mil/news/story.asp?storyID=123005347 (accessed 6 February 2006).

Haas, Lt Col Christopher. To the author. Letter, 18 February 2004.

Hallion, Richard P. *Storm over Iraq: Air Power and the Gulf War.* Washington, DC: Smithsonian Institution Press, 1992.

Harding, Luke. "Battle for Afghanistan: Taliban Who Came Back from the Dead." *Observer*, 2 December 2001.

Hawkins, William R. "Iraq: Heavy Forces and Decisive Warfare." *Parameters* 33, no. 3 (Autumn 2003): 61–67.

———. "What Not to Learn from Afghanistan." *Parameters* 32, no. 2 (Summer 2002): 24–32.

Headquarters Allied Forces Southern Command. "AFSOUTH Fact Sheet: Operation Deny Flight." http://www.afsouth.nato.int/operations/denyflight/DenyFlightFactSheet.htm (accessed 5 February 2004).

Headquarters US Air Force/XPXT, Transformation Division. *The USAF Transformation Flight Plan, Fiscal Years 2003–2007.* http://www.oft.osd.mil/library/library_files/document_129_Transformation_Planning_Guidance_April_2003_1.pdf (accessed 6 February 2006).

Hinen, Col Anthony. "Kosovo: The Limits of Airpower II." *Air and Space Power Chronicles*, 16 May 2002. http://www.airpower.maxwell.af.mil/airchronicles/cc/hinen.html (accessed 16 February 2004).

Hirsh, Michael. "Blood and Honor." *Newsweek*, 2 February 2004, 38.

Hosmer, Stephen T. *Psychological Effects of US Air Operations in Four Wars, 1941–1991: Lessons for U.S. Commanders.* Santa Monica, CA: RAND, 1996.

Jalali, Col Ali Ahmad, retired. "Afghanistan: The Anatomy of an On-going Conflict." *Parameters* 31, no. 1 (Spring 2001): 85–98.

Jinnette, James. "Employing an Air Maneuver Force: Battlefield Air Operations with Surface Maneuver in a Joint Campaign." Research Report. Maxwell AFB, AL: Air Command and Staff College, 2003.

Joint Publication 1-02. *Department of Defense Dictionary of Military and Associated Terms,* 1 April 2001 (as amended through 31 August 2005). http://www.dtic.mil/doctrine/jel/doddict/index.html and http://www.dtic.mil/doctrine/jel/new_pubs/jp1_02.pdf (accessed 6 February 2006).

Kagan, Frederick. "War and Aftermath." *Policy Review,* August–September 2003, 3–27.

Karsh, Efraim. *The Iran-Iraq War: A Military Analysis.* Adelphi Paper Series, no. 220. London: International Institute for Strategic Studies, 1987.

Keaney, Thomas A., and Eliot A. Cohen. *Gulf War Air Power Survey: Summary.* Washington, DC: Government Printing Office, 1993. https://www.airforcehistory.hq.af.mil/Publications/fulltext/gulf_war_air_power_survey-summary.pdf (accessed 31 January 2006).

———. *Revolution in Warfare?: Air Power in the Persian Gulf.* Annapolis: Naval Institute Press, 1995.

Kelly, Jack. "Iraq Provides Peacekeeping Institute with Needed Boost." *Pittsburgh Post-Gazette,* 27 November 2003.

Khalilzad, Zalmay, and David Ochmanek. "Rethinking US Defense Policy." *Survival,* Spring 1997, 43–64.

Kugler, Richard L., Michael Baranick, and Hans Binnendijk. "Anaconda's Lessons for Joint Operations." Defense and Technology paper. Washington, DC: Center for Technology and National Security Policy, National Defense University, 2006.

"Kurdish Resistance Forces Must Decide Role in New Iraq." *Washington Post,* 13 May 2003.

Lambeth, Benjamin S. *Air Power against Terror: America's Conduct of Operation Enduring Freedom.* Santa Monica, CA: RAND, 2005.

———. *NATO's Air War for Kosovo: A Strategic and Operational Assessment.* Santa Monica, CA: RAND, 2001. http://www

.rand.org/pubs/monograph_reports/MRI1365/index .html.

———. *The Transformation of American Air Power.* Ithaca, NY: Cornell University Press, 2000.

Lichbach, Mark Irving. *The Rebel's Dilemma.* Ann Arbor, MI: University of Michigan Press, 1995.

Macgregor, Douglas A. *Transformation under Fire: Revolutionizing How America Fights.* Westport, CT: Praeger, 2003.

Mason, Maj Doug, USMC. "A New American Way of War?: Identifying Operational Lessons from American Involvement in Southwest Asia, Kosovo, and Afghanistan." Naval War College paper. Newport, RI: Naval War College, 4 February 2002.

McElroy, Robert H. "Afghanistan: Fire Support for Operation Anaconda: Interview (with) Major General Franklin L. Hagenbeck." *Field Artillery,* September–October 2002, 10–14.

Moore, Harold G., and Joseph L. Galloway. *We Were Soldiers Once . . . And Young: Ia Drang—The Battle that Changed the War in Vietnam.* New York: Random House, 1992.

Moseley, Lt Gen T. Michael. *Operation Iraqi Freedom: By the Numbers.* Shaw AFB, SC: Combined Forces Air Component, Assessment and Analysis Division, 30 April 2003.

Mouer, Capt Joseph M., USA, commander, ODA 064, C Company, 2d Battalion, 10th Special Forces Group. Memorandum for record, 27 April 2003.

Murray, Williamson, and Maj Gen Robert H. Scales Jr. *The Iraq War: A Military History.* Cambridge, MA: Belknap Press of Harvard University Press, 2003.

Myers, Gene. *Joint Aerospace Power: A New National Strategy.* Arlington, VA: Aerospace Education Foundation, 16 September 1998. http://www.aef.org/pub/eaker/jap.asp (accessed 28 December 2004).

Nalty, Bernard C. *Air Power and the Fight for Khe Sanh.* Washington, DC: Office of Air Force History, 1973.

Nardulli, Bruce R., Walter L. Perry, Bruce Pirnie, John Gordon IV, and John McGinn. *Disjointed War: Military Operations in Kosovo, 1999.* Santa Monica, CA: RAND, 2002.

Naylor, Sean D. "Nightmare at Debecka." *Army Times* 64, no. 10 (29 September 2003): 14–16.

Newman, John M. *JFK and Vietnam: Deception, Intrigue, and the Struggle for Power.* New York: Warner Books, 1992.

Nichols, Dave, Center for Army Lessons Learned. To the author. Letter, personal correspondence, 8 March 2004.

Nordeen, Lon O. *Air Warfare in the Missile Age*. 2nd ed. Washington, DC: Smithsonian Institution Press, 2002.

Olsen, John Andreas. *Strategic Air Power in Desert Storm*. Portland, OR: Frank Cass, 2003.

Parker, Danny S. *To Win the Winter Sky: The Air War over the Ardennes, 1944–1945*. Conshohocken, PA: Combined Books, 1994.

Pelletiere, Stephen C., and Douglas V. Johnson II. *Lessons Learned: The Iran-Iraq War*. Carlisle Barracks, PA: Strategic Studies Institute, US Army War College, 1991.

Pirnie, Bruce, RAND Analyst. To the author. Letter, personal correspondence, 29 January 2004.

Pirnie, Bruce, R., Alan Vick, Adam Grissom, Karl P. Mueller, David T. Orletsky. *Beyond Close Air Support: Forging a New Air-Ground Partnership*. Santa Monica, CA: RAND, 2005.

Press, Daryl. "The Myth of Airpower in the Persian Gulf War." *International Security* 26, no. 2 (Fall 2001): 5–44.

Priest, Dana. "A Decisive Battle that Never Was." *Washington Post*, 19–21 September 1999.

———. "In War, Mud Huts and Hard Calls," *Washington Post*, 20 February 2002, final ed.

Reese, Lt Col Timothy R. "Precision Firepower: Smart Bombs, Dumb Strategy." *Military Review* 83, no. 4 (July–August 2003): 46–53.

Ricks, Thomas E., and Doug Struck. "US Troops Coordinating Airstrikes." *Washington Post*, 31 October 2001.

Rip, Michael Russell, and James Hasik. *The Precision Revolution: GPS and the Future of Aerial Warfare*. Annapolis: Naval Institute Press, 2002.

Roberts, Kenneth Lewis. *The Battle of Cowpens*. Philadelphia: Eastern Acorn Press, 1981.

Romjue, John L. *From Active Defense to AirLand Battle: The Development of Army Doctrine, 1973–1982*. Training and Doctrine (TRADOC) Historical Monograph Series. Fort Monroe, VA: Historical Office, US Army TRADOC Command, June 1984.

Rosenau, William. *Special Operations Forces and Elusive Enemy Ground Targets: Lessons from Vietnam and the Persian Gulf War.* Santa Monica, CA: RAND, 2001.

Rostker, Bernard. "Transformation and the Unfinished Business of Jointness: Lessons for the Army from the Persian Gulf, Kosovo and Afghanistan." In *The US Army and the New National Security Strategy,* edited by Lynne E. Davis and Jeremy Shapiro. Santa Monica, CA: RAND, 2003.

Scales, Robert H., Jr. *America's Army in Transition: Preparing for War in the Precision Age.* Army issue paper no. 3. Carlisle Barracks, PA: Strategic Studies Institute, US Army War College, 1999.

———. *Certain Victory: The US Army in the Gulf War.* McLean, VA: Brassey's, 1994.

———. *Firepower in Limited War.* Rev. ed. Novato, CA: Presidio Press, 1995.

———. *Yellow Smoke: The Future of Land Warfare for America's Military.* Lanham, MD: Rowman and Littlefield, 2003.

Schmitt, Eric, and James Dao. "Use of Air Power Comes of Age in New War." *New York Times,* 24 December 2001.

Shaver, Maj John W., III, USA. "Office of the Strategic Services: Operational Groups in France during World War II, July–October, 1944." Master's thesis, US Army Command and General Staff College, Fort Leavenworth, KS, 1979.

Sterling Publications Group Media Public Ltd. Company. "Global Hawk High Altitude, Long Endurance Unmanned Reconnaissance Aircraft, USA." http://www.airforce-technology.com/projects/global/ (accessed 5 May 2006).

Staudenmaier, William O. "A Strategic Analysis." In *The Iran-Iraq War: New Weapons, Old Conflicts,* edited by Shirin Tahir-Kheli and Shaheen Ayubi. New York: Praeger, 1983.

Steed, Brian. *Armed Conflict: The Lessons of Modern Warfare.* New York: Ballantine Books, 2002.

Stewart, Richard. *Operation Enduring Freedom: The US Army in Afghanistan, October 2001–March 2002."* Paper. Center of Military History Publication 70-83-1 Series. Washington, DC: US Army Center of Military History, 2004.

Sun Tzu. *The Art of War.* Translated by Ralph D. Sawyer. Boulder, CO: Westview Press, 1994.

Swiecki, Capt Joe T., USA, commander, ODA 063, C Company, 2nd Battalion, 10th Special Forces Group. Memorandum for record, 21 April 2003.

———. To the author. E-mail, 17 February 2004.

Tatum, Kenneth. "The Impact of All-Weather Precision on Escalation Dominance." Student paper. Maxwell AFB, AL: School of Advanced Air and Space Studies, 2003.

Treacy, M. F. *Prelude to Yorktown: The Southern Campaign of Nathaniel Greene, 1780–1781.* Chapel Hill: University of North Carolina Press, 1963.

The United States Strategic Bombing Surveys (European War) (Pacific War). Reprint, Maxwell AFB, AL: Air University Press, 1987. http://aupress.au.af.mil/Books/USSBS/USSBS.pdf.

US Department of Defense. *Conduct of the Persian Gulf War: Final Report to Congress.* Washington, DC: Government Printing Office, April 1992.

———. "Operation Iraqi Freedom Military Deaths since May 1, 2003 (as of September 30, 2006)." http://siadapp.dior.whs .mil/personnel/CASUALTY/OIF-Deaths-After.pdf (accessed 23 October 2006).

———. "Operation Iraqi Freedom Military Deaths through April 30, 2003." http://web1.whs.osd.mil/mmid/casualty/OIF-Deaths-Before.pdf (accessed 7 March 2006).

———. "2003 Annual Report on the Military Power of the People's Republic of China, Executive Summary." http://www.4law .co.il/Lea1.pdf (accessed 10 March 2004).

US Department of the Air Force. *The U.S. Air Force Transformation Flight Plan.* Washington, DC: Pentagon, Future Concepts and Transformation Division, November 2003. http://www.af.mil/library/posture/AF_TRANS_FLIGHT_ PLAN-2003.pdf (accessed 8 March 2006).

US Department of the Army. *United States Army: 2004 Army Transformation Roadmap.* Washington, DC: Office of the Deputy Chief of Staff, Army Operations, Army Transformation Office, July 2004. http://www.army.mil/references/ 2004TransformationRoadmap/4%20ATR%202004Sum .pdf (accessed 9 March 2006).

US European Command Web Site. "European Command Leadership." http://www.eucom.mil/english/Command/Commanders.asp (accessed 8 March 2006).

US Government Accounting Office (GAO). *Operation Desert Storm: Evaluation of the Air Campaign.* Washington, DC: GAO, June 1997.

US House. *Statement by MG (RET) Robert H. Scales Jr., House Armed Services Committee, United States House of Representatives, 21 October 2003.* 108th Cong., 1st sess., 2003. http://www.house.gov/hasc/openingstatementsandpress releases/108thcongress/03-10-21scales.html (accessed 6 February 2006).

US Special Operations Command. *Special Operations Forces in Operation Iraqi Freedom, May 2003.* MacDill AFB, FL: US Special Operations Command, 2003.

Vego, Milan. "What Can We Learn from Enduring Freedom?" US Naval Institute *Proceedings* 128, no. 7 (July 2002): 28–33. http://www.usni.org/Proceedings/Articles02/PROvego07 .htm (accessed 29 October 2003).

Vick, Alan, David T. Orletsky, John Bordeaux, and David A. Shlapak. *Enhancing Air Power's Contribution against Light Infantry Targets.* Santa Monica, CA: RAND, 1996.

Weir, Fred. "Iraqi Defeat Jolts Russian Military." *Christian Science Monitor,* 16 April 2003.

White, Paul K. "Airpower and a Decade of Containment." *Joint Force Quarterly,* no. 27 (Winter 2000–2001): 35–39.

Woodward, Bob. *Bush at War.* New York: Simon and Schuster, 2002.

Zinni, Anthony. "How Do We Overhaul the Nation's Defense to Win the Next War?" Lecture. Marine Corps Association and US Naval Institute Forum 2003, Arlington, VA, 4 September 2003. http://www.mca-usniforum2003.org/forum03zinni .htm (accessed 13 October 2003).

Airpower, Afghanistan, and the Future of Warfare

An Alternative View

Air University Press Team

Chief Editor
James S. Howard

Copy Editor
Debra H. Banker

Cover Art and Book Design
Daniel Armstrong

*Composition and
Prepress Production*
Mary P. Ferguson

Quality Review
Darlene H. Barnes

Print Preparation
Joan Hickey

Distribution
Diane Clark

www.ingramcontent.com/pod-product-compliance
Lightning Source LLC
Chambersburg PA
CBHW031257280526
45784CB00004B/1888